Peace with All

Akbar
The First Interfaith Mogul King

By

Ana Perez-Chisti, Ph.D.

Copyright © 2022, Sufi Universal Fraternal Institute, Ana Perez Laflamme
The Sufi Universal Fraternal Institute is a 501c3 non-profit organization dedicated to the study of Comparative World Religions. Classes are offered on a regular basis and open to all people for the purpose of furthering understanding and respect for the many spiritual traditions. Please see the following website for more information.
https://sufiuniversalfraternalinstitute.live
sufimovementusa@gmail.com

Edited by Shams Kairys
Cover Design by Robin Julien Laflamme
Press by Krishna Copy
Production by Sufi Movement International USA
Production Assistant Robin Julien Laflamme
Copyright©2015 Ana Perez-Chisti
ISBN: 978-0-692-37483-2
All rights reserved. No part of this book may be reproduced, stored in a retrieval system, or transmitted in any form or by any means electronically, mechanical, photocopied, recorded or otherwise without expressed permission from Ana Perez-Chisti

Dedication

To Pir-O-Murshid Hidayat Inayat Khan for his loving service toward the Sufi Message of Spiritual Liberty and to my devoted husband Robin Julien Laflamme for his ardent support and to all Sufis worldwide who hold aloft the transformation of the heart. To my son, Adam Randall many thanks for his technical encouraging support and especially the Cheragas and Cherags who spread the Message of Unity. May you all be truly blessed.

Acknowledgements

Many thanks to Shams Kairys who edited the original manuscript and who offered advice; to Zoë & David GuthuWild for technical support; Kristin Fein for editorial review; to Sri Karuna Mayee who inspired my research during my visit to the Sri Aurobindo Ashram in New Delhi, India; to my husband, Robin who helped in all matters of technical and artistic support and to all my University students and Sufi mureeds who voyaged through the journey of Emperor Akbar's life and understood Akbar's ultimate transformation transmitted by the great Sufi Masters.

Peace with All
Akbar-The First Mogul Interfaith King

Contents
Dedication
Acknowledgements
Forward

Preface

    Platonic and neo-Platonic Influences; Akbars' Religious Experiment; Dealing with Spiritual Leaders; The Conquering Warrior Archetype; Reasons for Studying Akbar's Life History; The Sufis Influence; Abdul Fazl, the Court Historian; Arguments about Akbar; Akbar the Leader

Chapter I
    Akbar's birth and Early Years..1

Chapter II
    Boyhood..2

Chapter III
    Early Teen Years and the Spiritual Influence of the Sufis...........14

Chapter IV
    Akbar the Warrior..25

Chapter V
    Late Teen Years-Akbar's Sexual Appetite....................................29

Chapter VI
    Pilgrimage, Marriage and Courtly Intrigue..................................32

Chapter VII
    Akbar's Mature Years..35

Chapter VIII
    Recollection and Imperial Responsibilities.................................41

Chapter IX
    Gujarat..50

Chapter X
    Mission to Bengal..52

Chapter XI
    The Din-i-Illahi at Fatepur Sikri..57

Chapter XII
    The Jesuit Christians...68

Chapter XIII
    Spiritual Authority and the Mahzer...78

Chapter XIV
    Final Departure from Fatepur Sikri..88

Chapter XV
    Conclusion-Akbar's Legacy...99

Peace with All

Akbar: The First Mogul Interfaith King

CHAPTER I

Akbar's Birth and Early Years

He was born Abdu'l-Fath Jalal ul-Din Muhammad Akbar in the month of October 15th 1542 in a small town composed of less than five thousand inhabitants called, Umarkot (sometimes spelled Amarkot). The town was located in the sand-hills of the Sind desert adjoining what is now known as Rajputana. Because he was born in the time of the full moon his, Muslim father, Humayun, named him Badr-ud-Din (Full Moon of the Region) but his fifteen-year-old Muslim mother, Hamida Banu Begum wanted him to carry the name, which reverenced her father, Sheikh Ali Akbar Jami. Thus, was chosen as Jalal-ud-Din (Splendor of Religion), which gave a predestined impulse to the ideals, which Akbar was to attain in his lifetime. He was expected to carry the mission of his paternal lineage going back to Akbar's grandfather, Babar who was the direct male descent of Timur (Tamerlane), and thirteenth male born through the lineage of Genghis Khan, who was the first in the line of Mongolian conquerors.

There were many mystical occurrences surrounding Akbar's entire life but most importantly during his early years, there were miracles that came in the form of protection. The fact that Akbar lived after his birth was a miracle in itself as the region near Jodhpur was under the rule of Rana Maldeo, a powerful and malicious prince who wanted to capture all travelers, particularly Moguls, who were regarded as Indian Muslims. Fearing retribution, Humayun and Hamida Banu decided not to travel out of the area, and stayed under the protection of Rana Virsal Prasad in Amarkot where safety was guaranteed for themselves and their child.

The relationship between Humayun and Rana Virsal Prasad proved to be an important alliance in view of the politically motivated murder and revenge that Rana Prasad's enemy, Shah Hussain, had earlier perpetrated upon the Rana's father. Humayun marched with Rana Prasad's army seventy-five miles southwest of Amarkot and regained the lost kingdom that belonged to him. It was at this time that Akbar was born.

The gift of a son, particularly arriving during a conquest, was indeed auspicious to Humayun. A generous distribution of food and sweets were sent to the population of Amarkot. Being of very superstitious disposition, when news arrived to Humayun that a son was born to him; he prostrated himself on the ground in joy and reverence, and in supplication he asked for continual Divine protection. Although he was torn and wanted to return to his wife to share the great blessings of Akbar's birth, he stayed at the battle front focusing on winning the territory for Rana Prasad. He considered a delay of thirty days as a self-inflicted state of renunciation, before seeing his newborn son. As a symbolic gift to the courtiers, and to show the legacy that Akbar was to carry into the future, Humayun sent a vial of musk, which was broken open upon a plate and distributed to the many Amirs with the following words.

> "Circumstances do not permit me to be more lavish. I restrict myself to presenting to you this token gift in the hope that the fame of the infant prince [will] spread throughout the world like the fragrance which fills the air of this tent."[1]

As Humayun moved his troops against Shah Hussain's forces, Humayun's army grew by the addition of many straggling individuals ready to join his cause as he reached the district of Jun. As surrounding districts began to fall to Humayun without resistance, he began to feel that his wandering days were over. He was finally at home. He set up tents several miles outside of Jun and began courtly meetings filled with music, dancing and celebrating with wine and soma. Finally he sent for his wife and son at last and in true spiritual acknowledgment for Akbar's presence, the proud parent distributed alms to the degree never before known in Jun.

---

[1] Lal, 1913. P.6
[2] Fazl. (Vol. I.) 1973, 1977. Pgs. 69-128.

After the arrival of Hamida Banu Begum with their new son, Humayun decided to call in all the famous astrologers of the region to cast Akbar's chart. He was determined to coordinate several systems of astrology garnered from the ancient Muslim and Hindu calculations, which took many years. Historical documents recount Akbar's early days, to which Abul Fazl, Akbar's devoted historian, dedicated several complex chapters in his biographical accounts of Akbar's life. In the chronicled history, the Akbar Nama [2] there exist several chapters detailing and confirming that Akbar was indeed born under an auspicious star. In the Muslim casting he was born under the sign of Scorpio in the third house, "signifying the grant of dignity, glory, greatness and magnificence.[3] In the Hindu system he was born under the sign of Leo, which was declared, "Significant of perfect supremacy, victory, energy and superiority."[4]

The Shirazi astrologer Maulana Fatuehullah came from Agra in 1583 and configured his chart, which was later recorded by Maulana's Chand and Ilyas. The Hindu astrologer, Pandit Jotik Rai had cast a chart as well. Humayun, out of respect for the two great master astrologers, was determined to reconcile the two different systems for the benefit of his son's destiny. Humayun's idea to recocile both charts proved an auspicious choice that influenced Akbar's actions later in his reign. The collective chart reading indicated that the child Akbar-born into the signs of propitious fortune, future father of many children, future leader of great armies, and future conqueror of new territory-this child was destined to be a messenger to the world of perfect reason and justice.

Filled with the joy of his son's birth, Humayun once again was forced to handle the impending storm gathering outside his camp at Jun. Although the Rana urged him to take on the conflict with Shah Hussain, Humayun gave no response. Disturbed by this, the Rana cut off all relations with Humayun, demanding that his army return to Amarkot. When Humayun refused, the Rana's army deserted him. Now isolated, the Moguls found themselves in a perilous situation. An alliance had to be reached with Shah Hussain

---

[2] Fazl. (Vol. I.) 1973, 1977. Pgs. 69-128.
[3] Ibid. P.75
[4] Ibid. P.85.

immediately so Humayun could find safe headquarters to reconoiter. Humayun and his retinue left Sind for Baluchistan in 1543.

CHAPTER 2

Boyhood

In Baluchistan the early boyhood years of Akbar's life was politically uncertain and complex. Humayun became embroiled in many confrontations that took him from his family. These political conflicts and absences caused acute emotional distress for Hamida Banu Begum. Becoming more fearful and uncertain, she remained withdrawn from Akbar. The lack of parental supervision and the natural precociousness of such a brilliant child opened up opportunities for Akbar to explore new experiences such as small rebellions from authority. For example, he refused to read and write although he could express himself eloquently at an age when most young children are known to babble. To cope with emotional abandonment, he began to test himself with dangerous physical experiences such as wrangling with poisonous snakes with his bare hands, and riding wild animals. These feats, later in his life, became legendary. His uncommon intelligence and physical prowess might have been the fictitious tales of servants and sycophants of the sitting Emperor but they lead us to the awareness that Akbar's unusual daring were of a miraculous nature. Because so many incidents of his unusual behavior were recorded it supported Humayan's belief that Akbar was indeed the incarnation of the great saint, Khwaja Ahmad Jam, who came to Humayun in a dream three years prior to Akbar's birth and told him not to lose heart as good fortune was to come to him.

Abul Fazl records evidence of the great saints reincarnation. One evening, as the story conveys, Jiji Anaga, Akbar's nurse, said that he had conveyed to her, when he was eight months old, the following statement:

> "Akbar looked intently at my face, turned around to make certain no one else was in the room, and suddenly spoke. 'Be of good cheer, for the celestial light of the *khalifat* [the eminent proponents of the Prophet's will] shall abide in thy bosom and shall bestow on the night of thy sorrow the effulgence of joy. But see that thou reveal this secret to no one, that thou doest not proclaim untimely this

mystery of God's power, for hidden designs and predications are contained therein.'" [5]

Jiji kept this occurrence secret until Akbar attained the throne in 1556. It was conveyed to Abul Fazl who entered it into the biographical work, The Akbar Nama, years later. There were always many stories in the court of Akbar's exceptional qualities and he was beginning to show more of them to his parents. His parent who prized his presence had little time to dote over Akbar. Humayun was beset by continued trouble in the region, aggravated by Humayun's brother, Mirza Kamran.

Unrest in the region was demoralizing the population. Mirza Kamran who was Humayun's bitter foe, aggravated by betrayal in the past, had won the Western portion of Babar's empire thus thwarting Humayun's desire to move through Baluchistan to Qandhar. A miraculous turn of protective events occurred. Mirza sent troupes into Humayun's camp to capture him and Hamida Banu, but as warning of this coup came early through a well placed spy, they safety fled to the hills in the northwestern regions known to be difficult to traverse.

They sought the protection of Shah Tahmasp of Kazvin, Persia and left Akbar behind in the Palace with clear instructions to the servants to give him to Mirza Askari, another tribal chief who worked in agreement with Mirza Kamran but still remained in friendly alliance with Humayun. Upon seeing the child, Askari's heart softened and he vowed to look after him, and brought him to Qandhar to his wife Sultan Begum, a very religious and wise woman. Akbar formed a deep relationship with Sultan Begam, and he maintained devoted to her throughout his life. She was perhaps the first mother in whose arms he felt safe and nurtured. For eighteen months Akbar, nearing his third birthday, flourished under her watchful guidance and loving embrace. Her devoted religious nature was one of the major factors that later inspired Akbar's spiritual pursuit for truth.

---

[5] Fazl, (Folio 187), and Lal, 1980, P.16

The year that Humayun and Hamida Banu spent with Shah Tahmasp was ordained by destiny to be an important influence not only in Humayun's life, but consequently effecting Akbar's artistic choices in later years. Shah Tahmasp was a cultured man of high intelligence and he respected the master artisens of his period. He was famous for gathering artisians of the Mogul school of Indian painting around him as well as musicians and poets. Shah Tahmasp, who held his throne for twenty-three years, was the second most powerful ruler in the Safavid dynasty,[6] as the son of Sultan Haider, he had a direct lineage to the great Shah Ismail.[7] The Shah's position and manner impressed Humayun greatly as the Shah's nightly court concerts were of the most exquisite refinement of sound and beauty he had ever heard or seen. A great friendship and trust ensued between the two men and the Shah became openly sympathetic to Humayun's situation.

When Akbar was three years old, Humayun advanced on Qandhar with fourteen thousand troops given to him by Shah Tahmasp. For safety, Akbar was removed from the palace and taken to Kabul and given to Khanzada Begum, Babar's elder sister and most senior royal lady in the region. Akbar did not see his father again until the later part of that year when Humayun led the conquering army into Kabul. At last his father was in possession of the kingdom he desired for so long. He made effective contacts with the majority of Afghan tribal chiefs, and his declaration of amnesty pleased the Afghan people. Hamida Banu arrived another year later to the jubilance of young Akbar.

After another attempted coup masterminded by Humayun's brother, Mirza Kamran, threatening to overtake Kabul, a counter offensive had to be waged to stop him. The conflict became very brutal and became viewed as a vendetta between brothers. Out of revenge, Mirza Kamran ordered a spy to sneak into Khanzada Begum's quarters and abduct young Akbar. The three-year old child was then brought to the battlefield and exposed to cannon-ball fire and soldiers being slaughtered. While the brutal scenes of

---

[6] The Safavid Dynasty was a merger of Turkish and Iranian Shia population spearheaded by the Persian Sufi mystic Sheikh Safi al-Din (1252-1334) based in Ardabil in northwestern Iran.
[7] Shah Ismail transferred the Timurid school of painting from Heart to the Safavid capital of Tabriz.. As a patron of the arts he set up a royal library for the production of the famous Shahnameh (Book of Kings).

battle were waging in the narrow passes surrounding Kabul another miracle by Akbar is described by Abul Fazl:

> "When this evil act (the exposure of Akbar to violent war) was practiced, the hands of the marksmen trembled, the arrows flew crooked, and the stock of steel and stone congealed. Sambal Khan, master of the imperial artillery felt his ardor grow cold and wondered what had happened to him. He also noticed with surprise that the shots of musketeers known for their accuracy were going far off their mark. Everyone noticed this miracle. When Sambal Khan looked at the ramparts of the castle, his vision quickened and he recognized His Majesty the child Shahinshah Akbar. The horror of the sight almost drove the souls out of the bodies of the gunners, and they all became listless. In a moment, he ordered the firing to stop. Wherever God's protection stands sentinel over His chosen one, what power has human stratagem to do him harm ?"[8]

Seeing his brother's ploy to harm his son, Humayun became more determined, and tightened his grip around Kabul. Mirza Kamran fled quickly, knowing his brother would now kill him without mercy, which would have been the normal code of the Timurid warrior toward another of the Timurid line.

Humayun was so happy at his son's survival of such a brutal environment at so young an age that he rewarded him and his caretakers with rich honors. Although Abul Fazl never mentioned the shock of these circumstances on such a young boy, the scenes horrendous scenes of battle haunted Akbar all his life and would take exteriorization in his violent behavior. This experience could easily be a major reason for Akbar's addictive and debilitating behavior in later years.

But the time Akbar turned five years old he appeared confident, warrior-like in his manner, and lived in true imitation of his father and grandfather Babar. What made him more exceptional at this period of his life was that he had already memorized works of

---

[8] Lal, 1980, P. 30

Hafiz and Sa'adi that he had heard recited. Persian and Turkish Sufi scholars were now returning to Kabul, but despite the efforts of the royal mentors, Akbar appeared to be incapable of learning to read or write. He averted scholastic study at every turn. Even when Humayun tried to bring in Maulana Assamuddin Ibrahim, an eminent scholar and several other celebrated men such as Sheikh Bayazid and Maulana Abdul Qadir[9], to provide Akbar's education, all efforts failed. The only exception was the liberal tutor, Mir Abdul Latif Quzwini, who was the first person to introduce Akbar to the principles of *Sulk-i-kul* (peace with all), his was the only influence that was congenial to the young pupil.[10]

Even in the presence of a fine tutor, Akbar wanted only to face the joys of danger and physical challenge. He loved being outside in nature and he rebelled continuously against being held indoors to the regret of his mentors. Humayun and Hamida Banu Begam fretted over the consequences of Akbar growing up illiterate, but Akbar's astrologers comforted Humayun with these words.

> "He will be wiser than the wisest of his age. His knowledge will however, come from within himself. His sagacity will be rooted not in books, but in divine inspiration. Your majesty may send him to school, but the august prince is a school unto himself. Neither Sa'adi nor Hafiz has much to teach him. He himself is destined to be the teacher of mankind."[11]

With great-unresolved enmity between the two brothers, many battles ensued between Mirza Kamran and Humayun. In the year 1551, when Akbar was nine years old, Humayun decided to take Akbar on his military campaign to fight against his uncle. This was beyond a doubt the most eventful occasion in the course of the young Emperor's life, one that would set the course for his military conquests in the future. The many majestic elephants that transported arms, the weaponry, the soldiers armour, the grandiosity of the

---

[9] Blockmann, 1871, 1965. P. 614. Maulana Abdul Qadir of Sirhind was one of the most learned scholars of Akbar's reign and a great Sufi master.
[10] Krishnamurti, 196, P.5
[11] Ibid. P.32

large number of men in the entourage moving under one command, all fascinated him. He was absorbed completely in the visceral experience of the campaign.

Akbar was not only allowed to take part in all the councils of war but he was encouraged to express his views and implement suggestions. He made many friends among the soldiers and developed loyal officers to whom he offered suggestions. He would walk around the camp to see that his suggestions were followed. He was a keen observer and a born helmsman.[12] He began to feel comfortable and respected in this environment and enjoyed the camaraderie of the men.

The theater of battle, the grandeur of war, and the contest of military strategy made their mark on his being and became an outlet for his unresolved emotions. He loved animals and observed the courage their raw nature expressed. He preferred spending hours in a dusty soldier's mobile tent-city, filled with the scents of war, to following his studies in the palace. He remained defiant against his tutors, and disappointed Humayun and Hamida Banu many times. It was natural that they wished for a well-schooled scholar to rule the empire and follow the learned line of his great grandfather, Umar, and grandfather, Babar. Akbar's parents did not realize how their son's perceptive eye was taking in more than just the military maneuvers; he was absorbing the psyche of the warrior and watching for fidelity among the men. These aspects of the human personality were more important to him than learning from books.

Loyal to his father and fascinated by the conflict with his uncle, he witnessed how Mirza Kamran came to a torturous end. After his capture, Mirza Kamran's eyes were plucked out and his only wish was to end his days in Mecca. The torture of his uncle left an indelible mark on Akbar that haunted him later in life. This treatment went against the Timurid code of warrior behavior, where an enemy is respected for his valor. The elder religious councilmen (*'ulama*) tried to explain how a traitor must be justly dealt with, particularly after perpetuating assaults on his own family. They tried to justify their comments with complex dictates of right and wrong, punishment and beneficence quoted

---

[12] Ibid. P.42

from sacred writings of the Holy Qur'an and *Sunnah,* but Akbar would have no part in it. His logic came from an intuitive awareness as the astrologists had confirmed to his father. He would advance a new ethic born from insight into human relationships. Akbar believed, even as a youth, that the universal spirit controlled human affairs and that all beings must be dealt with justly. He held this belief throughout his days. Akbar listened earnestly to the pundits reasoning, but he felt that redemptive torture was not sacrosanct as law nor should it remain unchallenged.

Akbar, now thirteen, began in earnest his lifelong quest to think outside the cultural box. The confined assessments of morals, laws, and religious beliefs expressed by those around him were constantly being reassessed and analyzed. He had a prodigious memory, and he tried to apply reason and clear justice to all his actions. The ideals of justice were borne on the wings of two master Sufi giants, Hafiz and Sa'di, whose writings Akbar memorized and cherished. Hafiz gave guidance as to what a King must do for others, he said,

> "There seems to be a great reward
>   For clear thinking:
> All existence is a pawn in the Friend's hands.
> Look, one gets wings and gifts to the world
>   Music each morning;
> One turns into such an extraordinary light
> He actually becomes a sustainer of a whole planet,
> One makes a thousand moons go mad with love
>   And blush all night
> When one can surrender the illusion, the crutch of
>   Free will,
> Though still live –for the benefit of others—
>   The highest of moral
>   Codes.[13]

---

[13] Ladinsky, 1999, P.113, 114.

Sa'di offered the road map of spiritual surrender through his own humble being, saying,

"O King! Deck not thyself in royal garments when thou comest to worship: make thy supplications like a darwesh, saying: 'O God! Powerful and strong Thou art. I am no monarch, but a beggar in Thy court. Unless Thy help sustain me, what can issue from my hand? Succour me, and give me the means of virtue, or else how can I benefit my people?'"[14]

The two Sufi masters were always close to Akbar in thought and heart affinity, and he tried to assimilate the deeper awareness that the Sufis were know to illicit in their own methodology of mystical transformation while he was still in warriorship training.

In the beginning of summer 1554 Humayun's most faithful commander, Bairam Khan, known as Khan-i-Khanan, observed how Akbar's subtle observations of military strategy were uncanny, that they were always accurate and highly reasonable. Inspired by his most trusted commander's comments, Humayun took Akbar with him on his military campaign to Lahore. Humayun, still true to his father Babar's past actions, had placed a pyramid of bodies in the middle of Panipat. During this conquest, Humayun emulated his Mogul father's practice of ordering thousands of severed bodies to be raised as a victory memorial in the middle of the town-square. Humayan like Babar believed in retribution. This action sent a strong message to the surrounding community to cease all rebellion, and indicated that one from the dynastic Timurid line was now in charge. The way was now open for the conquest of Delhi to finally be achieved, and he entered the city victorious in the end of summer 1555.

Akbar deplored the idea of stacked up body parts as a sign of victory and held aloft a different standard for the victorious accomplishments worthy of a warrior. Wishing to save the village people from the plunder of the defeating soldiers by interceding in the raid, he asked his father to call an amnesty declaration instead. Prayer was emphasized

---

[14] Edwards, 1805, P.27

and alms were given to all. Akbar's strategy deflected cruel pilfering by the soldiers of the conquered community and rather made them appear as heroes. Generosity was the element of surprise no one expected.

Humayun was so deeply impressed by Akbar's humanitarian requests that he gave him the province of the Punjab to rule. Little did he know that Akbar's placement would be the most important political installation of his final days. Within months, while Akbar was stationed in the Punjab, Humayan fell down a flight of stairs in his library and was dead within two days. In the next year, on February 14, 1556, at the ripe age of fourteen years, Akbar was crowned Emperor at Kalanaur. This moment is described in the <u>Tarikh-i-Akbari</u> with supreme accuracy.

> "He who sits under the protection of God, he needs not fear even if the whole world becomes his enemy. On Friday, Rabi-us-Sani, A.H. 963/February, 1556 A.D. Nawab Khan-i-Ali Shah, Muhammad Bairam Khan, known by the title of Khan-i-Khanan, and holding the high office of the tutor, together with other leading nobles of Emperor Humayun placed Khaqan Akbar, the eldest son who had completed fourteen years like the moon of the 14th and had rise to the fourth sky, on the throne of kingdom, at the town of Kalanaur, which is a suburb of the capital city of Lahore, and made him the crown of the imperial throne. Thus the height of fortune, good luck and pride kissed the feet of the liberal king." [15]

With this step into Imperial authority, Akbar began earnestly to contemplate methods of justice in a new light, he began to reflect on improvements and prosperity for the betterment of his subjects. He took his newfound authority with great seriousness, and regarded his role as being a messenger of change and beneficence.

---

[15] Muhammad Arif Qandhari's Tarikh-I-Akbari P.44. This historical document was compiled during Salim (Jahangir's) reign and is considered one of the authentic comparative and independent sources of information outside of Akbar's court recorder, Abul Fazl.

CHAPTER 3

Early Teen Years of Akbar's Reign and the Spiritual Influence of the Sufis

Wars were still being waged in Agra, Lahore and on the outskirts of Delhi. Hemu, a military genius was succeeding on the battlefield with unchallenged victories over Hindustan. He had set himself up as a sovereign on his own volition and held his territory in the northwestern part of Hindustan. Although Hemu was considered to be born of low birth from the Hindu slums of Riwari, he amassed a faithful following and practiced highly pragmatic principles in the service of the Afghans, namely the Sur family, under Islam Shah. However he was beset with weaknesses that caused him to indulge in lust-filled pleasures and display unprovoked acts of cruelty unlike any seen in the ancient world. When people would come out of their houses to greet him, he would shoot golden arrows into their heads and kill them on the spot. During a battle, as fate would have it, Hemu was struck in the eye with an arrow and taken prisoner. His decapitated head was sent to Kabul and his body hung at the entrance gates of Delhi. While such an atrocious end might be fitting for a warlord preceeding Akbar's reign, Abul Fazl suggests that Akbar, "who was trying to illuminate justice," [16] had nothing to do with the manner in which his enemy was treated. Even though Hemu's life reflected choices fit for a despot and were vulgar in regards to all standards of military comportment, Akbar distanced himself from redemptive violence.

With Hemu dead, the end of the hundred and four years of rule of Hindustan by an Afghan dynasty was in sight. The road to Delhi was now clear, and on November 6th 1556 Akbar saw his entry into Delhi not as a conquest but as a homecoming. Still not fully independent in his choices, and holding true to his father Humayun's Mogul modeling, Akbar believed that certain types of behavior were expected of him. Although thoroughly repulsed by this type of barbaric behavior, he placed a pyramid of body parts in the center plaza announcing the presence of another Timurid who had come to power.

---

[16] Fazl, (Vol. I), P. 618

Akbar's forefathers were not in harmony with that of Akbar's humanitarian disposition. Yet the encoded patterns of the victorious Timiruds continued for a while longer.

However caught Akbar was between the old patterning and his new ideas, the perceptive members of his court could see a new and changing perspective beginning to form, particularly in the way he treated his mother and other women in his court. Unlike other monarchs of his stature, when Hamida Banu Begam came to join his court in Delhi, Akbar threw himself at her feet while declaring great joy and excitement and embracing the woman who gave him birth. Because he showed this selfsame respect and unique display of affection for his other mother, such as Sultan Begum, he won the hearts of many of his courtiers simply by this guileless act of boyish and spontaneous affection. These primary women who influenced his character could be credited, along with his tutor, Mir Abdul Latif Quzwini, for forming the foundations of Akbar's policies of tolerance (*sulk-i-kul*) that would take effect in his later years.

In the early 16th century, men matured earlier, died younger, and took upon their shoulders heightened responsibilities even in their teen years compared to those men found in contemporary societies. It should be noted that the expectation for a child to perform highly focused and responsible duties at such a young age was the cause of great psychological pressure. The complexities of being an Emperor were mounting daily and stressing Akbar's natural youthful development and rebellious. Political issues compounding around the vicinity of Delhi added pressure by his generals for his mature counsel. This caused a reaction of aversion as he moved away from the guidance of others. Expected to perform to the highest standards of his role, he began to feel isolated and alone. The greatest feeling of desolation came with the betrayal of his trusted tutor Bairam Khan who had been Humayun's trusted Vakil. This break in their relationship was caused over the choice of women Akbar wanted to marry, a nineteen-year-old beauty and daughter of Mirza Abdullah Khan Mogal. Bairam Khan was opposed to this marriage due to the family connection to Mirza Kamran, as he felt the alliance would open jealousies and inter-family conflict bringing back upon Akbar all the problems Humayun suffered. Akbar took umbrage to Bairam Khan's opposition, and he began to chafe under

Bairam Khan's religious bigotry. The Khan hated the Shia population and Akbar knew it. Along with this added tension, Akbar's growing sexual needs were beginning to grip him and predominate over his reason. His sexual desires were going to become a source of great turmoil for him for the rest of his days, bringing unforeseen trouble and conflict to his reign as Emperor. The Khan could see that Akbar was becoming uncontainable, and yet he held his ground even more rigidly.

Akbar continued to feel torn about the Khan-i-Khanan's lack of approval and support. He had been a counsel and trusted guide to Babar as well as his father Humayun. Although Bairam Khan had logical reasons for his opposition to this marriage, Akbar went ahead with the marriage and the link with his tutor's guidance was severed forever. To justify his disappointment in the advisors who opposed him, he would take journeys into the forest alone to be with animals. Akbar always felt he learned more about life from experiences with animals than from people, whom he felt were always suspect in their motives. At this time in his life, he did not have the capacity to see from Bairam Khan's perspective and factor his opinion into his own decisions. Akbar's autonomy needed room and time to expand, and he felt the elder counsel members were inhibiting his ability to perceive insightfully his own voice with demands often rooted in orthodox religious protocol.

At this time of deep challenge, Akbar had an experience with a horse that proved to be a powerful teaching.

> "In this period of solitude he mounted upon this suspicious steed and set off rapidly, leaving society aside and increasing his glory by the presence of God. When he had gone some distance, he dismounted for some purpose and, becoming heedless of the nature of his steed, assumed the posture of communing with his God. That shifty and fiery horse acted according to his custom and rushed off rapidly so that it disappeared from the far-searching gaze of His Majesty. When his holy heart was again disposed to mount, there was no one in attendance, and no horse at his service. For a little while he was perplexed, not

knowing what to do. Then suddenly he saw that this very horse was coming from a distance and galloping towards him. It ran on till it came back to him and stood quietly waiting for him. His Majesty was astonished, and again mounted the noble animal. God be praised! What apprehension can there be from solitude to him who the incomparable deity favors, and of whom he takes charge?" [17]

Akbar understood this experience with the fiery horse as a sign that the Divine was with him and favored him, and he did not have to give over his will and reason to another. The independence and insight that Akbar yearned to achieve when alone and in deep conversation with God were confirmed. He realized he had to move away from the counsel that reflected the past. He had once valued his tutor above all else but now he had to value his own intuition and inner guidance and look into the future with brave audacity. Even though Bairam Khan had risen to a distinguished position through his long years of dedicated service to his grandfather and father, a breech between them had severed the trust he once held. Also, the fact that Bairam Khan favored Shiites over Sunnis caused distress for Akbar. In negotiations the Hanafi *'ulama* were the privileged of all religious leaders in the land, [18] and equality and fairness were not a priority for the Bairam. So, when the break became particularly marked because Bairam Khan did not favor Akbar's first of many marriages to the daughter of Mirza Abdullah Khan Mughal, a falling out was inevitable. Akbar was young, highly sexed, and emotional and he did not see the possibilities for inter-family hostilities, as did Bairam Khan. Now the major elements were in place for a big change in Akbar's life which were to greatly affect courtly arrangements that were formatted historically by his father and grandfather.

Akbar, now seventeen years old, having entered Delhi victorious, began setting up the foundations for his empire. He commanded large courtly celebrations and seized every opportunity for continuing the festivities. He believed the giving of alms was necessary and he favored setting up prayer ceremonies so that he could display uncontrolled outbursts in his devotional behavior. These types of events reflected his rebellion and

---

[17] Lal, Akbar, 1980 P.69
[18] Burke, 1989. P.109

persisted throughout his late teenage years. Akbar continued to refuse to learn how to read and write, but he was touched by the subtle impulses of heart-directed teachings in the Sufi art of poetry. He memorized many of the great Sufi masters, and their ideas seemed to surface as a rosy perfume when he needed it, bringing amazement at how deeply the Sufis words affected him.

At this time in his young years religious discussions were of little interest, only the more exteriorized display of wild devotional prayer seemed to free him from the burdens he was beginning to carry. But ideas were stirring deeply in his being and he was becoming more and more influenced by the Sufis who were richly populating the area. He was particularly attracted to the manner of the Sufis, as they did not preach or argue religious philosophy as pundits of different faiths were doing, but rather they were intent on manifesting the Divine qualities within themselves. This was exhibited by how they respected one another's differences and always related to each other in a manner befitting sacred recognition by saying in exuberant greetings, *"Ya Azim,"* meaning "The Greatest of all Beings," which acknowledged the Divine presence in those before them. He became deeply affected by how Sufis ruled out all intercession or mediation with the Divine and how they opened wide the gates of immediate spiritual communion with and in all creatures. Akbar could readily admire their manner (*adab*), and he began to inquire more deeply into their methods as he found resonance with his own feelings and experiences.

His book learning was meager but he memorized many more of the famous classical texts of his time. He demanded that classical texts be read to him often, and he listened intently for hours. He often surprised his tutors and members of his court with his spontaneous recitations from classical manuscripts that he could recite verbatim. His prodigious ability to hear and recite was rapidly developing as a keen talent to compensate for his illiteracy. This became his way of learning not only the great literary masterpieces of his time, but of retaining all discussions with infallible accuracy.

It was during these teen years that Akbar began to challenge the authorities of Islamic law (*mujtahids*). Akbar, opposed the blind following of those who held fast to Islamic theology, (*'ulama*) and whose religious policy stood directly against the ideas of tolerance, (*sulk-i-kul*) that he was beginning to formulate.[19] Akbar wanted to hear Hindus, Jains, Jews, Parsis, the Jesuit Christians and Zoroastrians freely speak about what they knew.[20] Akbar was truly what Max Mueller described- the first student of comparative religions. Not only did he show a desire to learn from the many religious teachings but he also began to consider the possibility that all religions are essentially equal in their dissemination of one truth.

This ideal was in accord with the Sufi teaching of "Unity of Being" (*wahdat al-wujud*), a spiritual ideal that integrated "essence" and "attributes" proposed by Al-Ghazzali in the 11th century.[21] Attributes such as knowledge, power, life, will, speech, hearing and sight were considered distinct from God's essence (*zat or dhat*), but co-eternal. The Sufis studied and distilled the works of 10th and 11th century Muslim philosophers such as al-Farabi[22] and Ibn Sina (Avicenna),[23] along with corresponding views found in Plato's Theory and Forms which distinguished between knowledge and mere opinion. Akbar was exposed to these philosophies during his father's reign. He was beginning to understand and synthesize the existence of absolute and changeless objects of knowledge, such as justice, holiness, beauty and equality. As these thoughts greatly appealed to him, he began to feel naturally drawn to the Sufis.

Pantheistic religious ideas, and other philosophical and mystical influences came to Akbar easily because he was exposed to and surrounded by some of the great Chisthi Sufi masters of his day. These were men of high caliber such as Sheikh Salim Chisthi, who was the son of the renowned Sheikh Musa, who appeared to be a simple village smith

---

[19] Alam Khan, 1999. P. 9
[20] Ibid. P. 13
[21] Abu Hamid Muhammad al-Ghazzali, (1058-1111) was a formative Persian Islamic philosopher who was well known in medieval Europe for his rationalistic theories that influenced Jewish and Christian thought.
[22] Abu Nasr al-Farabi (878-950) commented on the range of Aristotle's logical treatises and regarded his work as an integral part of Syriac and Arabic traditions.
[23] Avicenna (also known as Ibn Sina) (980-1037) contributed greatly to the aristotelian theology concerned with defending truths of faith that were laid down in the Qur'an. His ideas merged up as a school of philosophy in the Persian and Arabic worlds.

(*ahangar*) but who performed many miracles, as well as Mawlana Abd 'l-Qadir of Sirhind, who was considered one of the most learned masters of Akbar's age. They congregated in close proximity to his court and readily responded to his invitations to come and discuss religious matters.

Akbar's profound faith in the Sufi ideal of 'Unity of Being' (*wahdat-al-wujud*) was not surprising, as Sufi methods and philosophies were shared with him by his father who regarded the Sufis influence as constructive ethics for building a community. Humayun had been initiated by the Shattariyya Sufi Sheikh Phul (d.1539) and by Sufi Sheikh Muhammed Ghaus (d.1563). Akbar's great-great grandfather Umar Sheikh Mirza and great grandfather Babar had also been initiated by the Naqshabandiyya Sufi Order of Khwaja Ubaidullah Ahrar (d. 1490)[24]. Through this lineage, Akbar had been exposed early in his life to the Sufis mystical ideals, liberal religious attitudes and interiorization of practices. The Shattariyya focused on the coordination of heavenly bodies associated to human fate, and the Naqshabandiyya turned their hope of salvation to the promised deliverer, the *Mahdi*. For Akbar these ideas advanced his acceptance of the one truth found in the many faith systems without need for disputing doctrine. He began to work with the unity principles, which were also found in the exegetical works of the great Andalusian Sufi, Ibn al'Arabi (d. 1240). Akbar was also keenly aware of other Sufi ideals such as caring for the poor, and showing a divine manner to all beings (*adab*).

Without knowing it Akbar was an important influence on contemporary schools of Sufism which would arise in the West ten centuries later. As the Sufis method for unfolding the unique qualities in the individuals development, two processes later called, the art of personality and the unity of religious ideals were formulated by the Sufi Master Hazrat Inayat Khan, who founded the Sufi Movement International in Paris and Geneva in 1910.

Hazrat Inayat Khan's Sufi principles blossomed in the 20th Century as the Message of Love, Harmony and Beauty and synthesized the teachings found in four schools of

---

[24] Ibid. P 3.

Sufism: Chisthi, Naqshabandi, Suhrwardi and Qadiri. Such unitive methods brought dignity and nobility to the human spirit, which was struggling under the darkness of World Wars I & II.

As Akbar witnessed the mystical circles of dervishes sitting together in their tattered robes and honoring each other as representatives of the Divine manifestation, he was inspired to use the unitive principles for developing his ideas for greater tolerance (*sulk-i-kul*). He knew that the chief goal in the Sufi way of life was to find the revealed meaning (*batin)* hidden in the code of "divine oneness" (*tawhid-i-illahi*), and not stop at the external meaning (*zahir*). He found encoded harmonies in these teachings and became ecstatically moved by the Chisthi Sufis love of art and music as a means for attaining Divine Union. All the arts were felt to be giving evidence to the ineffable inner landscape made manifest through the Creator, and this interior spirituality Akbar understood innately. Art as spiritual practice was formed and instituted into the Chisthiyya Sufi Order in Ajmer by the revered Saint, Khwaja Moineddin Chisthi, whom Akbar remained devoted to all his life. He was exposed to the Sufis for many years of his youthful development and the Sufis were patiently guiding him to the direct apprehension of the Divine nature in all things.

Akbar sympathized with these Sufi methods because he had developed a great love of art, architecture and music. The integral legacy of Persian refinement lived in Akbar through his father Humayun, who had the opportunity to enhance his artistic appreciation while staying with Shah Tahmasp. Contemplating these effective and creative mystical methods of the Sufis, Akbar began to express his "high voltage" and rational individualism.

He believed he was to be a conduit to verify the truth of any religious theory through his experiences. The idea of experiential pragmatism was coherent in the Sufis method of practice, wherein they aligned their inner heart state by awakening the love of God that brought them into union with all creation. No one was exempt because of culture, cast or condition. Sufism was not just for the elite. Sufis were focused on embodying and encompassing both phenomenal existence and what was beyond existence.[25] They offered the unitive practices that held the Islamic community (*ummah*) together not through doctrinal fixity but by a heartfelt desire for solidarity, a natural extension of the ancient tribal loyalty that had generated an ethos of purity, honor and collective esteem. Akbar finally found a community of spiritual seekers in the Sufis who reflected his pantheistic ideals and who were living from an exalted and transcendent awareness.

Akbar continued to revere, as did many great leaders before him, the great Sufi saint, Khwaja Moineddin Chisthi, the 10th century 'Syrian' who was a descendant of the Prophet Mohammed (*SAAwS*). Khwaja (Master) was deeply admired by the many communities and different lineages of Sufis. He was an embodiment of simple living and noble thinking. Khwaja Moineddin exhibited great self-control and renunciation in matters of the flesh, and he gave himself selflessly to others showing great patience, perseverance and courage. He lived in continual states of meditation and contemplation, and was entirely free of avarice and greed. He sought nothing but the pleasure of God, and he was deeply committed to serving the downtrodden and the sick.

The Chishti community, originating at Chisht in Khorasan, founded a center in Ajmer, where they specialized in the use of music in their exercises. They felt that music sprang from the very beginning of creation, and was to be found in all areas of life such as in the waving of branches, the whistling of the wind, the sound of the sea and the flashes of lightning and thunder. The sounds of insects and other creatures, even the very breath, was a constant tone that could be understood by the listener in accordance with the highest perfection.[26] The wandering dervishes of the Order were known as "Chist" or "Chisht." They would enter a town and play a rousing air with a flute and drum to gather people round them before reciting a tale legend of initiatory significance. These methods of the Chisthis soon became crystallized into a simplified love for music.[27] Even today these musical methods are used by the Inayati orders of Sufis in Europe and North America.

---

[25] Ibid, P.17
[26] Hazrat Inayat. (Vol. II), 1960, 1969, 1970. Pgs. 89-92
[27] Shah, 1990, P. 127

Khwaja Moineddin was so loved and admired by his students, that after his death, they opened up a medical clinic at his burial site (*dargah*) in Ajmer offering treatment, free of charge. All people who came in need called by the Saint's legends were given a gift of healing and grace, which continues to this time. Khwaja's sainted teacher, Hazrat Khawja Usman Harooni (d. 617 A.H.) of Baghdad, was also revered for his enlightenment and great moral teachings illustrated through his actions. The Chisthis maintained an unbroken lineage of the most sublime ecstatic thought, methodologies of wakening the mind, and heart-centered ethics which were preserved and honored as they passed from teachers (*Pirs*) to their students (*mureeds*).

Khwaja Harooni admired his beloved *mureed* Moineddin and always spoke with great praise for his famous student saying, "He loved playing music and often he would fall into a state of rapture during a concert". Later after his illumination, Khwaja Moineddin believed that inner vision could be attained through the arts. Coupled with his generous disposition and hospitality to the destitute, he became a legend to all who were seeking the love of the Divine through the awakening of their hearts.[28] Khwaja Moineddin believed we are all teachers one to another and therefore we all have an obligation to love our community as our own family.

Many charismatic teachers arose in this lineage of teaching and Sufi convents (*khanqahs*) were formed as well as new Sufi Orders (*tariqahs*), all adding to the unity of the Empire, which Akbar would rule. The unity was enhanced because the khanqahs were a place of sharing information and building heart-based relationships. Through the process of meeting regularly and performing prayers, solidarity was the outcome. The Chisthi khanqahs followed the same friendly protocol and Khwaja Moineddin's fairness impressed Akbar deeply as he contemplated on Sufi ideals until he developed his own inner resonance with their methods. The legendary stories of Khwaja Moineddin's musical events, well attended by visiting dignitaries were so numerous, that his miraculous healing powers became legendary throughout the area around Ajmer. It was

---

[28] Sharib, 1961. 1967. 1975.

for this reason Akbar remained steadfast to the great saint by performing ritual pilgrimage almost every year of his life. The complexity of being a warrior-emperor and also a spiritual devotee to the unitive principles of the Sufis, were the essential battleground issues (*jihad*) of his inner-most struggle.

CHAPTER 4

Akbar the Warrior

As much as Akbar enthralled himself with Sufi studies, conflict was brewing on the outer provinces of Delhi and Akbar had to leave the evening sessions of music, mystical teachings, debate and stories about the great Sufi Saints and further test his skill again as a military leader. With Bairam Khan no longer functioning as Akbar's advisor and holding bitterness toward Akbar because he rejected his counsel, Bairam convinced Shah Abul Maali to become his partner in the hope of over-throwing Akbar's Imperial House. Historians collectively mention that although the Khan-i-Khanan's natural character was good and amiable, he fell into bad company and his natural good qualities were clouded by the flattery of sycophants[29] as well as a broken heart. For obvious reasons the Khan-i-Khanan's emotional preference was not in this battle to over throw Akbar. He felt broken by Akbar's rejection of his counsel and he had become arrogant. But he held a special place for this exceptional young boy who he admired and tutored and to his surprise, the emotional conflict with Akbar disabled his military ability. His loyalty to Humayun never altered yet he could not accept this type of rejection, which seemed as though he was being caste away from his own son and family.

Bairam Khan was still a swift and cleaver advocate of military strategy and a stance of opposition against him and his forces would have been bloody beyond measure, not to mention a possible defeat for Akbar. But now this action by Bairam against the son of his most honored Emperor Humayun brought him to despair which was revealed through his military vacillations in strategy. He would rest for days by the river, walking up and down in removed and agitated contemplation. His days were numbered as he wrestled with his ego to accept Akbar's offer to admit defeat. He perceived the offer as a

---

[29] Abul Fazl, Akbar. Pakistan: Sheikh Mubarak Ali Publishers and Bookseller. 1875, 1975. P.25.

weakening of his greatness and a degrading set back in his court position to the Emperor in the eyes of the world.

Akbar knowing that his once devoted tutor, was standing against him now with wishes to topple the very dynasty that he helped Akbar to build, was confusing and troublesome to Akbar's developing awareness. Although Akbar yearned for continual independence from any dominance, he would have preferred Bairam in his court as a favored advocate. In reverence to his tutor, he had his court scribes draft a letter to Bairam Khan in the hopes that he would unconditionally surrender and see the mistake in his undertaking. The letter gives insight to Akbar's developing ideas of fairness and application of Sufi principles, at the age of seventeen and reveals the depth of respect in which he esteemed his "Khan Baba."

> "Your services and your fidelity to this great family are known to mankind. It is a matter of great surprise and shock to us that you have chosen the path of warfare, and are intent upon damaging the grand empire you have helped build up. Both history and God will not forgive you for the crime you are about to commit. Because of the respect in which we hold you, the offer made to you earlier is still open. The commanders of our army are under instruction not to fire the first shot, but if you finally decide to use force they will have no option but to resist with every resource at their disposal.
>
> For many years, because of our tender age, we did not cast our glance on political and financial affairs, and all the business of sovereignty was entrusted to your excellent capacity and knowledge. Now that we have applied our own mind to the affairs of Government, it seems to us only right that you should respect our wishes and lend us your valuable support. To build an empire at once strong and prosperous is our common objective. We respect your wisdom and have faith in your loyalty. In our childhood we called you Khan Baba. Our attachment and deference for you remain unchanged. We have no intention to humiliate or dishonor you. Your surrender will be a victory for the values you yourself hold

dear. In this greatest of all your conquests, you will be honored both by God and your king.

Let me tell you, O revered friend of the family, that in the remote chance of our army suffering a setback at your hands, the Almighty Allah will record the blackest ever defeat in the ledger of your scores. It is not for us to give you lessons in moral behavior. You are the preceptor, the wise one of the age.

In reminding you of your obligations, we are only repeating what you yourself taught us time without number. We look forward to receiving you at the court with the honors due to your status." [30]

The letter reflects Akbar's deep feelings and his desire to favor Bairam. The Khan-i-Khanan did not wish to accept Akbar's request at first, he did eventually give in and came to Akbar's presence to ask forgiveness which he received. Akbar, in true respect, honored him against the better judgment of all those members in the court who encouraged him otherwise such as his foster mother, Maham Anaga who detested the Khan-i-Khanan. Maham Anaga's intention was ferociously directed toward advancing her son, Adham Khan, into that most lofty place, as Prime Minister, next to the Emperor. Perceiving herself the perfect lieutenant of the empire,[31] her continual pursuits in this venture caused great problems later for Akbar. She saw Bairam as one of the main obstacles in her plan to progress her son while neglecting to regard Adham's tyrannous and obnoxious personality.

Bairam, according to his request, wanted to live his final days out in Mecca. Leaving with honors befitting a great general, Bairam departed. During a stopping point in Gujarat, enemies of the Bairam stabbed and killed him on the street and left him to die like a commoner. No one knew until years later, when his bones were exhumed from a commoner's grave and identified, that this was the man who counseled three Emperors

---

[30] Lal,1980. Pgs 85,86.
[31] Srivastava, 1998, P.26

for decades. Akbar made sure he was given a dignified burial at last. In deep grief Akbar wept openly at his official entombment.

With no restraints to bind his decisions, Akbar felt finally unhampered by his advisors. He was free to marry his cousin whom Bairam refused to accept. Akbar married her after observing respectful days in mourning for Bairam. When the Emperor was very young he always knew that without the Khan-i-Khanan the salvation of the Mogul empire would be extinct. As Akbar was in his maturing years, in return for Bairam's fidelity, Akbar was generous and loyal to Bairam's family and children and supported them throughout his entire reign.

CHAPTER 5

Late Teen Years of Akbar's Reign

Akbar was now eighteen years old and entering upon his most rebellious period. Hunting wild animals in the daylight hours followed by exhaustive nights of revelry where wine and soma were being passed around freely made him even more reckless. Akbar knew that he was addicted to these substances as his father and his grandfather before him. As much as he could self-perceive, the schizophrenic states of numbness and hyper-activity exhibited by his father were now his condition. He understood the compelling effects these substances had on his nature yet he became helpless in their sway. He burned off the hostile effects of the drugs in his sports as well as in his lustful pursuits but he had an ambivalent response when faced with stopping the use of them. He used drugs and alcohol on a regular basis throughout his entire life, which later became the modeling influence that destroyed his sons and evaporated his legacy.

His addiction to mind altering substances caused predictable difficulties for the young Emperor as his libidinal forces quickly got out of control. He began, for example, to lust after the dancing girl who had been taken into the court of Baz Bahadur. Her name was Rupmati[32] and she was of such intoxicating beauty that poems and songs were spreading wildly around the empire and particularly in the area of Malwa where Baz Bahadur lived. Baz Bahadur was an acclaimed Hindustani vocalist and rose to the racks of "*ustad*." He was famous throughout Malwa for his ragas and ragnis and his love for Rupmati became legendary. His passionate songs and poems of love dedicated to Rupmati's beauty drove Akbar into jealous rages. Historically, if we follow and accept the accounts of Abul Fazl who calls Baz Bahadur an "arrogant, degenerate drunkard,"[33] it would prove to be untrue. Baz Bahadur was a disciplined and inspired artist living by the mastery of his creative genius. When the artistic side dominated his personality his affect on people was uplifting

---

[32] Blockman, (Lucknow ed.) P.274. Rupmati is sometimes spelled Rumpati in texts such as detailed by Firishta in his account of the rulers of Malwa.
[33] Fazl, (Vol II), 1977, P. 211

but when the fierce Tartar background that had earlier been developed in the area of Ujjain came to dominance, he trampled underfoot anything that came in his way.

These were wasteful and hideously misdirected years for Akbar. Images from hell-raising were in his imagination and he executed poor judgment in matters of state. War was usually waged for ideological causes, expansion of territory and dominance of trade routes, not over passing emotional states of jealousy or inebriated desires for an innocent dancing girl. He was a possessed man who had to own this female beauty who belonged to a man now deemed his enemy. He would get drunk and act offensively to all around him in frustration at the passion that was building inside of him to possess her. In the state of manic obsession Akbar invented a cause to go to Malwa and slaughter his opponent. With the help of the court sycophants around him and no elder to guide and control his appetites, Akbar concocted a plan to go to war. He conveyed the message that bringing peace to the harassed people of Malwa; living under the despotic reign of Baz Bahadur would now be brought under Akbar's humanitarian protection.

Baz was no ones fool. He knew of Akbar's attraction to Rupmati and ready to meet Akbar's challenge prepared the harem ladies of his court to be dispatched into other protective custody. He gave the men who were in charge of his concubine's instructions to kill all the women immediately if he lost the battle to Akbar.[34] He did lose the battle and he fled to the hills. Every woman's head in the harem of Baz Bahadur was severed. Oddly Rupmati did not succumb to several severe wounds right away before her capture by what Abul Fazl called the "army of fortune" [35] who arrived to save her and carry out Akbar's the orders so that he could have her for his own. She escaped his soldiers and died by taking poison while hiding in a far corner of the region.

The smoke from the pyres of burning female bodies filled the air in Malwa. Akbar was stunned by Baz Bahadur's action to have all the harem women killed. As Akbar stood in the room where Rupmati had taken poison; he quickly reassessed the atrocity. He debated

---

[34] Ibid. P. 213
[35] Ibid. P.213

within himself the reality of life and death, of God and the Divine manifestations and the transitory nature of the world itself.[36]

To deal with the emotional blow of lose and failure in achieving to gain the possession of the women he wanted, Akbar did what he always did, he isolated himself retreating into the forest and challenged himself against wild animals. Deeds of daring liberated his pent-up emotions and gained him wide spread fame. Although people's adulation pleased Akbar immeasurably, he was now a wild man on a quest. He did not seek out answers through religion but rather he was attracted to the men of faith, the Holy men who were known to live by their religious experiences rather than words, those that desired God alone. Again, he turned to the Sufis.

---

[36] Lal, 1980, P. 102

CHAPTER 6

Pilgrimage, Marriage and Courtly Intrigue

He loved the stories of the great Sufi Saint Khwaja Moineddin Chisthi and wanted to go on pilgrimage to his holy burial place (*Dargah*) in Ajmer to receive the inspiration that so many thousands who visited there had spoken of. The occasion was truly one of the most important experiences in Akbar's life. He appeared as a common, simple man on an important journey. He dressed in simple white garb, ate simply and walked many miles barefoot over difficult terrain. On the way and during the pilgrimage, he opened his heart to the many people who came to him to share the problems of their lives and he granted many acts of generosity offering boons of courtly positions and money.

It was around the same time he took another wife, a leading Rajput princess, Jodha Bai, who was to become his most prized advisor in palace life and intellectual liberalism. Her intellectual skill and deep realization of equanimity in war and peace coupled with her devotion to her illiterate Emperor made them an effective team. [37]

Jodha Bai offered Akbar many gifts of grace but most importantly she was a necessary ally to Akbar in the palace when his relationship with Maham Anaga was coming under strain. Maham Anaga was filling the cherished courtly position left by the Khan-i-Khanan. But her priorities where always focused on moving her son Adham Khan into her position or one of greater power. As much as Akbar experienced self-doubt and would partake of long bouts of drunkenness and spend inebriated nights with the many thousand women now in his harem, he could not eradicate his feelings of growing insecurity to run the empire by himself. He had become increasingly suspicious of those who equated responsibility with self-interest. Although he was often dealing with the disturbing side effects of drugs, his keen awareness into human motivation sharpened his

---

[37] Ibid. P. 105

senses to filter out those courtly members who desired to overthrow his power. He was now on hyper alert and he looked cautiously around his court for any spark of betrayal.

As a counter measure against the scheming of Maham Anaga's attempt to position Adham in ever growing powerful positions, Akbar appointed a trusted court elder to Maham Anaga's great surprise. Shams-ud-Din Muhammad Khan Ataka was given the post of Prime Minister on May 16th 1562. Shams-ud-Din was the husband of Akbar's wet nurse, Jiji Anaga and he was credited for saving Humayun's life in one of the battles they fought together. His term of service to the Emperor was short lived. The unscrupulous action for overthrowing Akbar's choice of Prime Minister to his court ended by the hand of Adham, who killed Shams-ud-Din by stabbing him to death in a dark hallway, when he left the Emperor's chambers. Adham conspired with Munim Khan, Ataka Khan, and Shahab-ud-Din Ahmed Khan, all cousins to Akbar, to carry out his directive's with the help of Maham Anaga.

It was not long before Akbar found out about the growing conspiracy. Devoted servants, overhearing information, would reveal to the Emperor the intricacies of the plot building against him. Soon it became evident to Akbar that he had to confront Adham himself. They met and fought and Akbar won the conflict by throwing Adham off the palace balcony, dragging him up the long palace stairway and throwing him out a second time, because the first fall did not kill him. Munim. Ataka and Shahab-ud-Din fled from the palace and disappeared.

Maham Anaga was so distressed at the loss of her son by so violent a death she died forty days later from grief aggravating other long-term disorders in her body. For Akbar, the complication of emotional factors arising in him about this kind of conspiracy led by those family members he trusted and loved were confusing and shocking. The lose of another mother who he always regarded as his primary caretaker and who was now to be regarded as a women who conspired to overthrow the very empire she helped him build added to his growing inward isolation.

He again used this event as an excuse to loss himself in long nights of drugs and drunkenness in the apartments of his harem. Abul Fazl, the faithful court historian, asks the pertinent questions about why other members of the court, who remained faithful to the Emperor, did not rise up and take action against the conspirators? Abul Fazl indicates that it could be due to the fact that Adham with the support of Maham Anaga had entranced so many with dreams of money and goods, they remained passive.[38]

Akbar always generous in victory like his father and grandfather before him forgave Ataka, Shams-du-Din and Munim. After they returned from hiding Akbar installed them into positions of courtly power. But a change had occurred in Akbar after this attempted coup d'état on his life and on his empire. With lose of trust in those he considered his family and swift evaporation of the innocent notions that his courtly family supported him, he matured from all notions of boyhood into a complete and independent ruler. He emphasized this fact by claiming in repetitive verbal declarations that reason was his guide. But Akbar's future years were bent on self-destruction and self doubt would plague his choices. His lack of ethical standards was at the very bottom of his sovereign station of functioning and this set the stage for the opposing forces within the religious *'ulama* that surrounded his court.

---

[38] Fazl, (Vol. II), 1977, P. 270

Tents

Instruments of battle

Clothing for the Emperor's Army

Map of Hindustan

Geneology of the House of Timur

10. Fathpur Sikri, Jodh Bai's palace, west side of courty[ard]

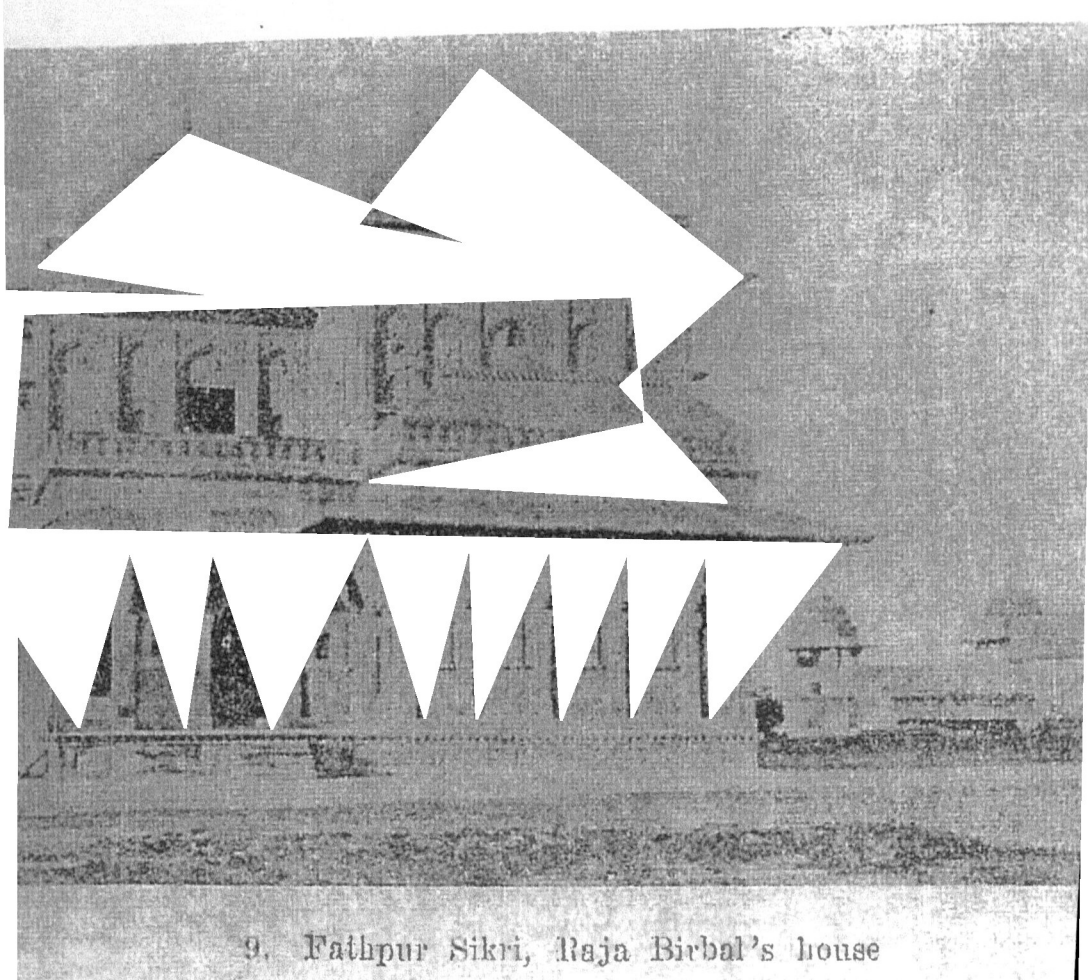
9. Fathpur Sikri, Raja Birbal's house

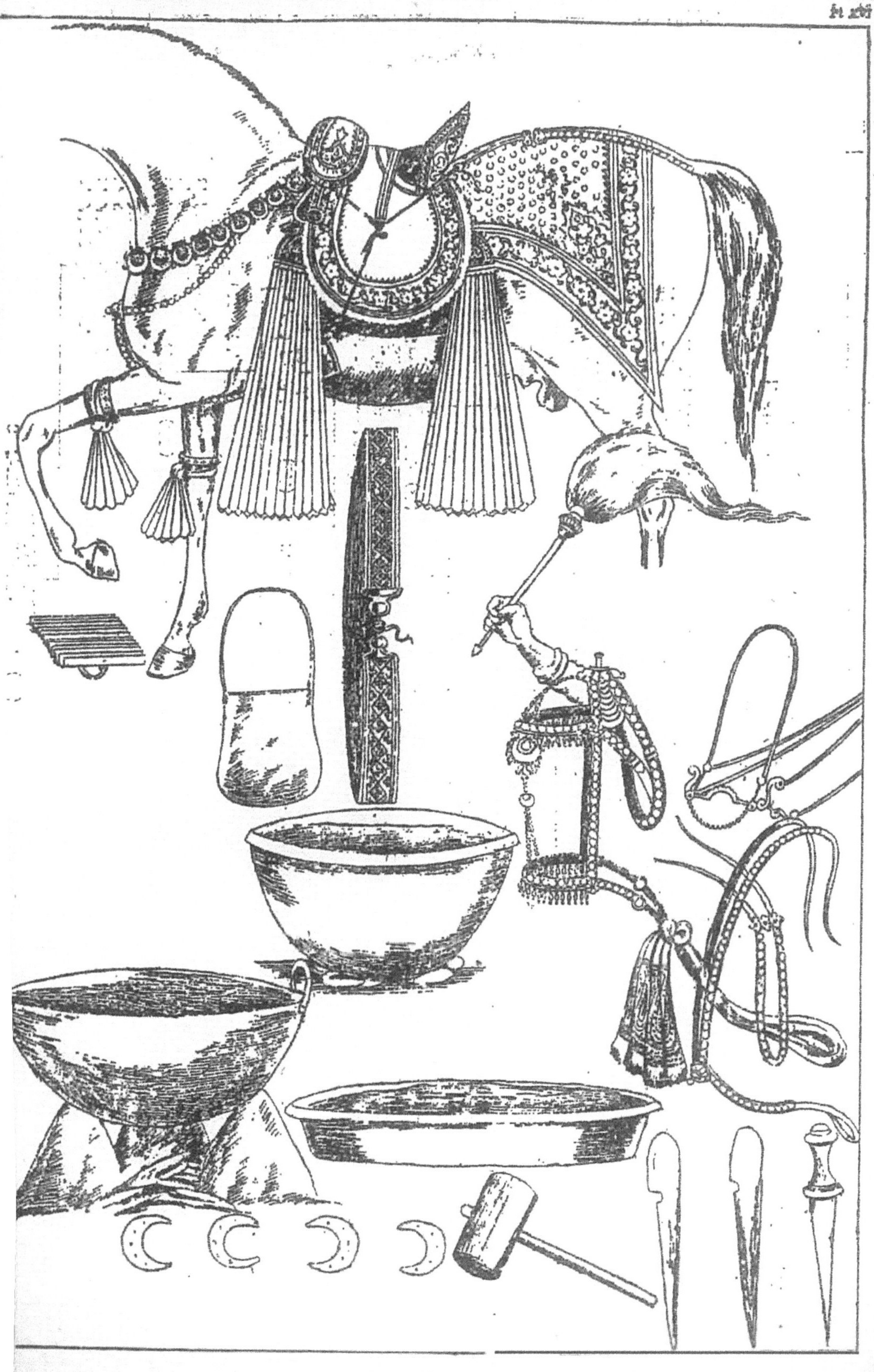

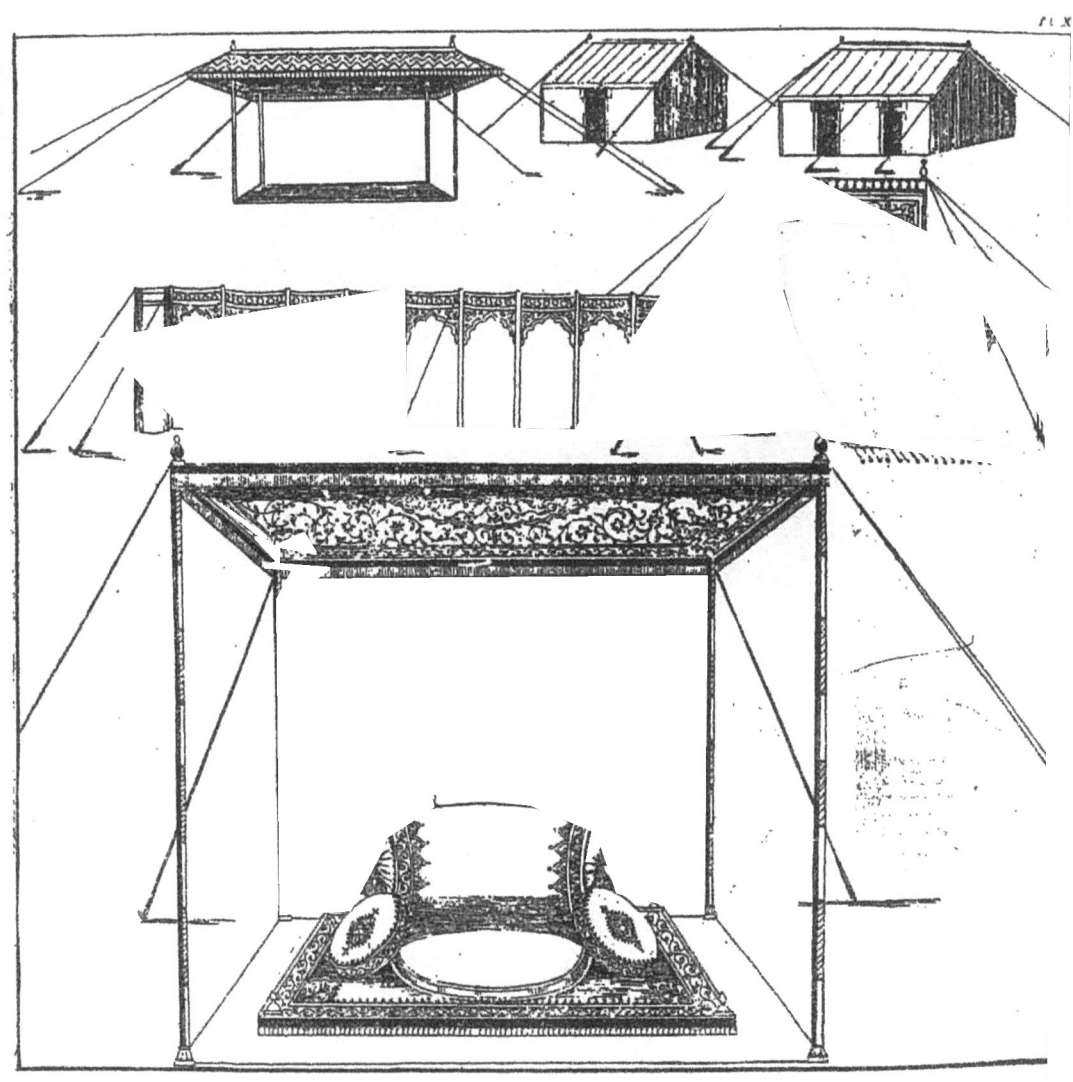

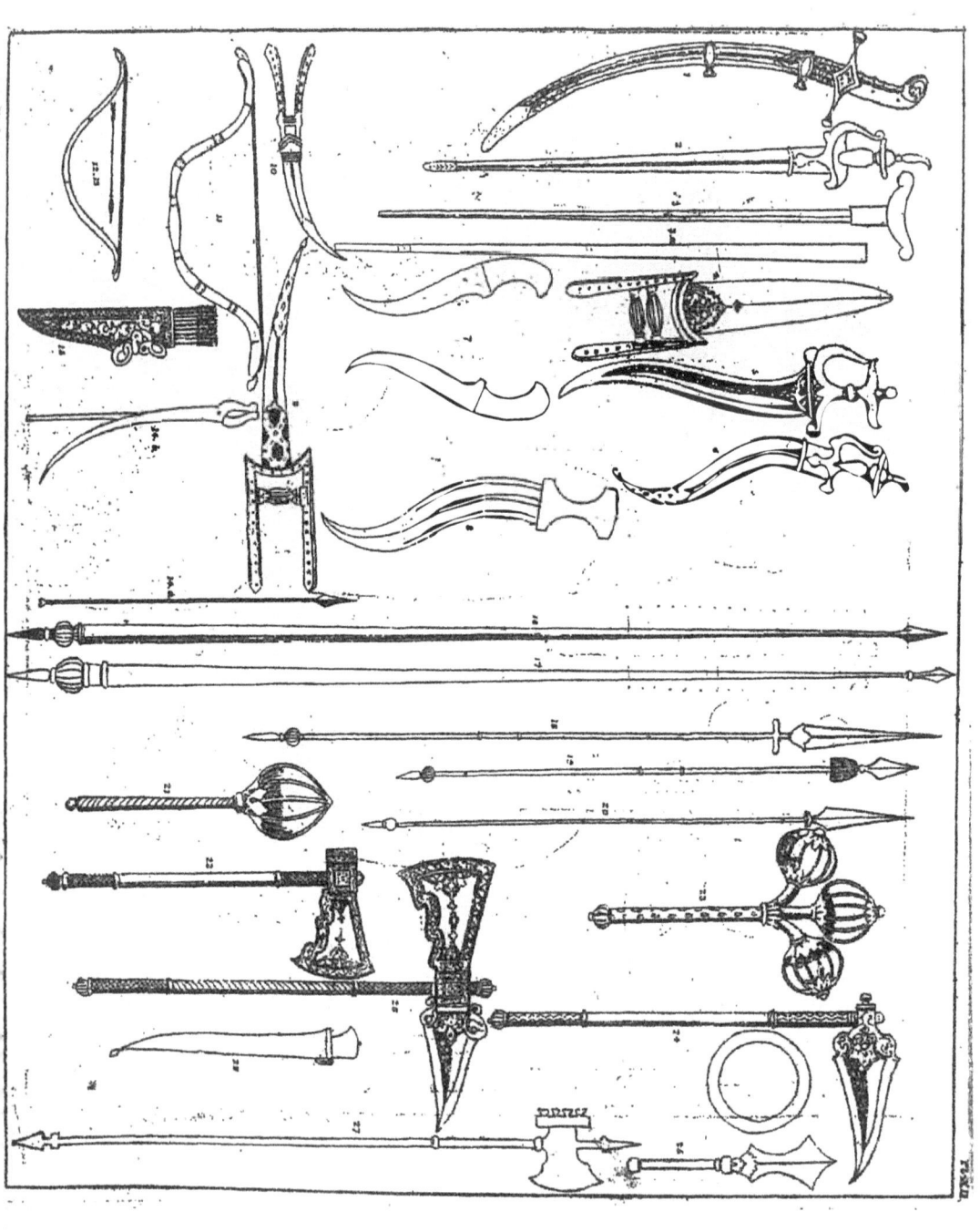

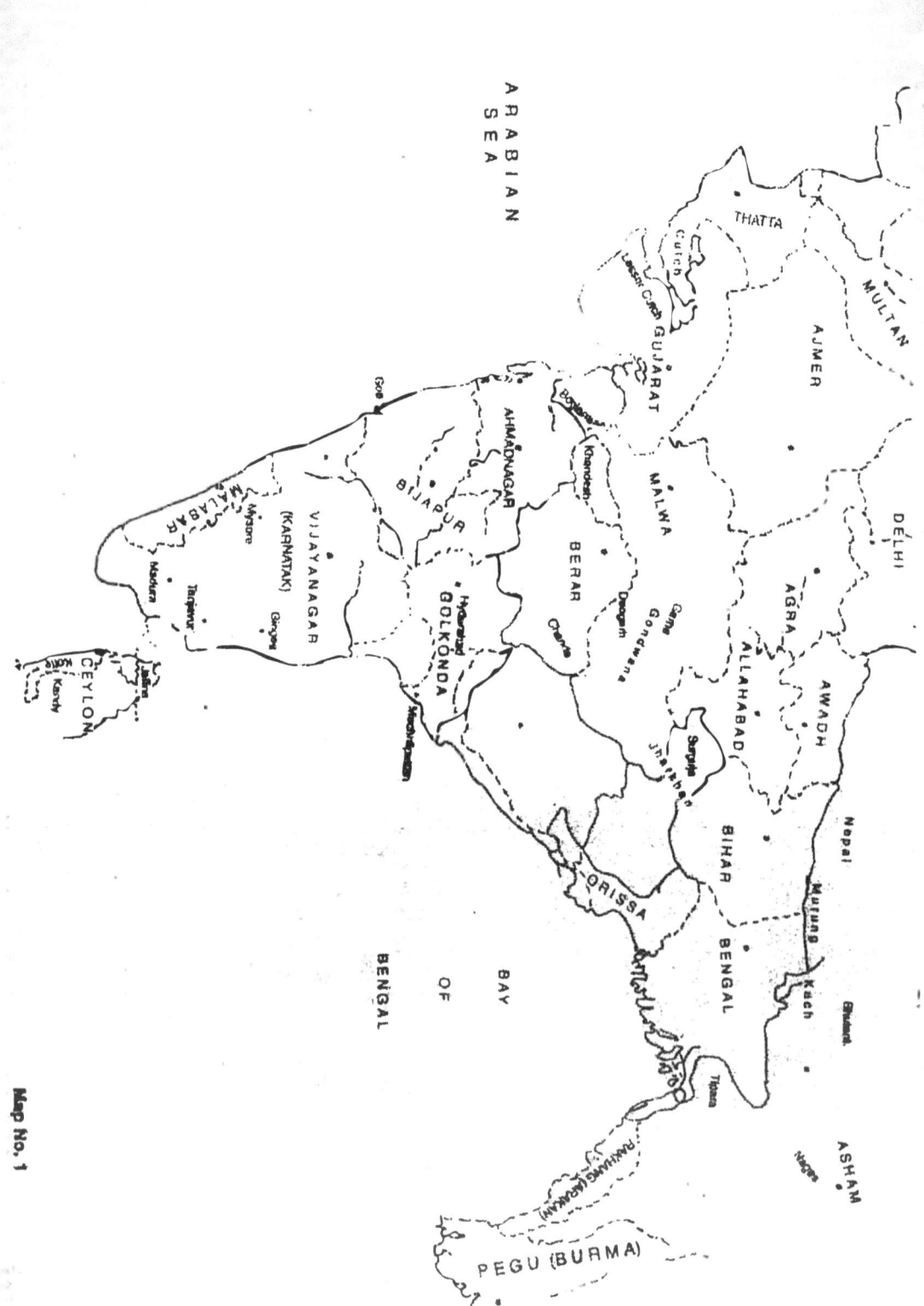

A GENEALOGICAL TABLE OF THE HOUSE OF TĪMŪR.
WITH SPECIAL REFERENCE TO THE MUGHUL EMPERORS OF INDIA.

Quṭbu 'd-Dīn Amīr Tīmūr Gūrgān (Ṣāḥib qirān-i aʿẓam), b. 736; d. 807 A.H. (I.)

3. Jalālu 'd-Dīn Mīrān Shāh. (II.)
b. 769; d. 810.

1. Abā Bakr Mīrzā.
2. Alangar Mīrzā.
3. ʿUsmān Chalbī.
4. Mīrzā ʿUmar.
5. Muḥammad Khalīl.
6. Sulṭān Muḥammad Mīrzā. (III.)
7. Ijil Mīrzā.
8. Siyurghtamash.

M. Sulṭān Masʿūd.

1. Sulṭān Abū Saʿīd Mīrzā. (IV.)   2. Minūchihr Mīrzā.
b. 830; d. 873.

1. Sulṭān Aḥmad M.   5. S. Murād M.
2. S. Muḥammad M.   6. S. Walad M.
3. S. Maḥmūd M.   7. Ulugh Beg M. (ruler of Kābul)
4. ʿUmar Shaykh M. (V.)   8. Abā Bakr M.
b. 860; d. 899.   9. S. Khalīl M.
                          10. Shāhrukh M.   ʿAbdu 'r-Razzāq.

1. Ẓahīru 'd-Dīn Muḥammad Bābar. (VI.)   2. Jahāngīr Mīrzā.   3. Naṣīr Mīrzā.
b. 888; d. 937. Titles, Gettisitānī, Firdawsmakānī.

1. Naṣīru 'd-Dīn Muḥammad Humāyūn. (VII.)   2. Kāmrān Mīrzā.   3. ʿAskarī Mīrzā.   4. Mīrzā Hindāl.
b. 913; d. 963. Title, Jannatāshyānī.
                                            Mīrzā Ā bū Qāsim.

1. ʿAbdu 'l-Fatḥ Jalālu 'd-Dīn Akbar. (VIII.)   2. Mīrzā Muḥammad Ḥakīm, king of Kābul; b. 961, d. 993.
b. 949; d. 1014. Title, ʿArsh-āshiyānī.

Ḥasan and Ḥusayn (twins).   3. Nūru 'd-Dīn Muḥammad Jahāngīr. (IX.)
b. 977; d. 1037. Title, Jannat Makānī.

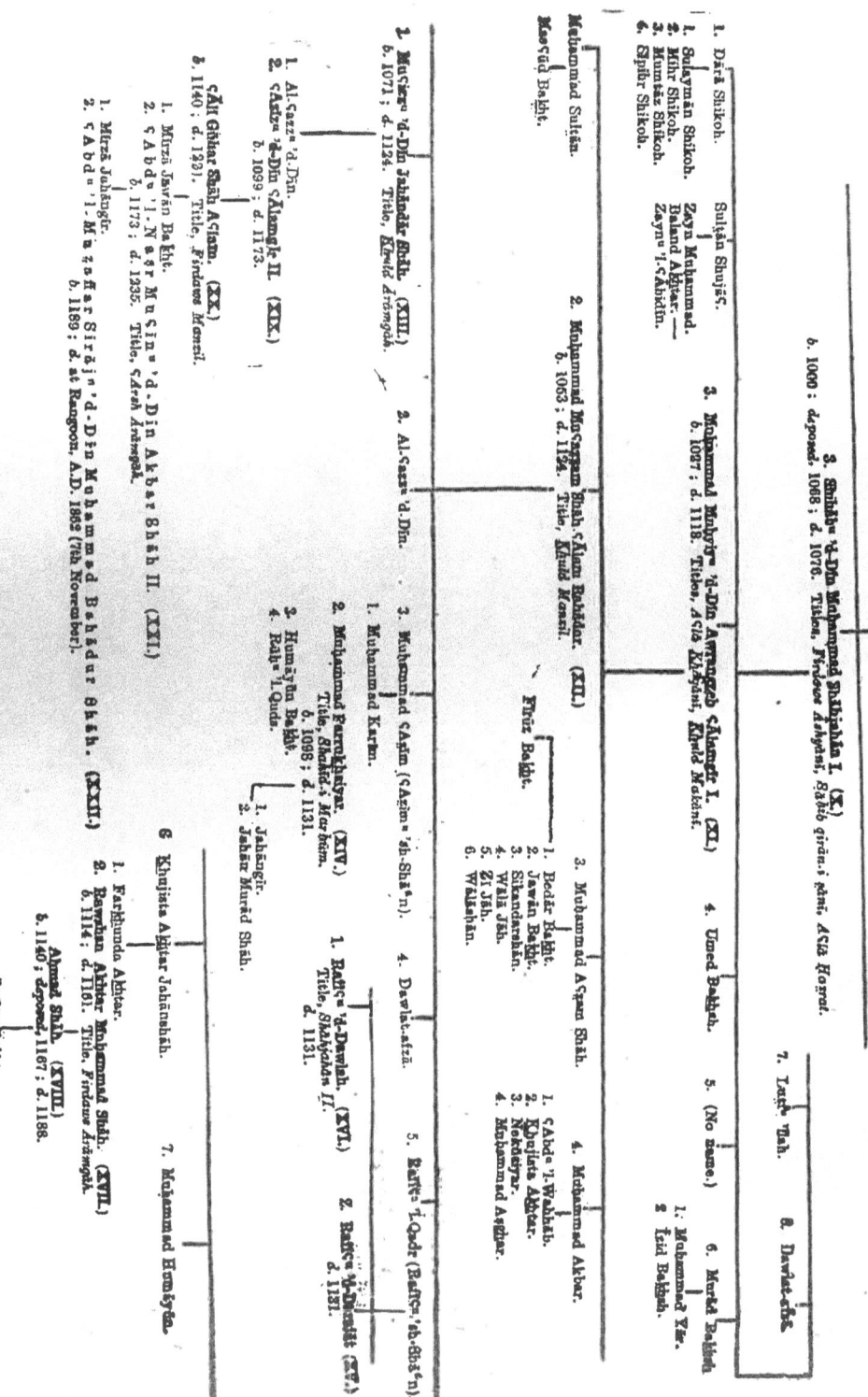

CHAPTER 7

Akbar's Mature Years

In 1562 Akbar now in his twenty- first year, under pressure from the '*ulama*, rekindled his search for the ideals he aspired toward that had been activated by his meetings with the Sufis. He began to leave his own pleasures and concentrate on the common interests of his people such as the need for education, particularly the study of languages, agriculture, and astronomy. He wanted proper buildings to support these community needs and he began to envision plans for designing a city. He wanted to provide jobs, reexamine rules of government, encourage medical practice and provide medical facilities while deepening investigation of the sciences. He wanted to open trade routes and markets of exchange so that dry goods, foods and spices would be freely available to all.

As passionate as he was about building this city, he was doubly passionate about the study of religion. He examined the critical stumbling blocks that impeded tolerance in many faith systems. He activated a strong effort to rid the empire of disabling prejudices that had been ensconced for centuries. Remembering the great teachings of religious tolerance taught to him by his stepmother Sultana Begum, and developed by the Sufis, he began to plan his altruistic steps. His goal was to sponsor a form of monotheism akin to what the Hanifs of Mecca, and the Prophet Mohammad (*SAAwS*) had once practiced. This effort would be Akbar's greatest accomplishment in his historic legacy.

Akbar's efforts were supported by two great movements in his time, one coming out of the Hindu religion, the other coming out of the Muslim religion.
Fifty years earlier two flourishing movements in India occurred at the same time, the Hindu Bhakti movement and Sufism. The seventh century witnessed the beginnings of Bhakti in Tamil-land in South India, while Sufism took root in Basra (now Iran), the hub

of the Islamic world.[39] The Bhaktis were ecstatic's and the Sufis were mystics and both sought truth and wisdom through union with God while focusing on the heart rather than the intellect. Sufism was spreading to Turkey, Central Asia, the larger area of Iran and India. The different Sufi orders flourished under the guidance of charismatic teachers (*Pirs*) one of them being Khwaja Moineddin Chisthi who Akbar deeply admired all his life. Akbar such as Hafiz and Sa'di also knew other great Sufi teachers and their writings were often recited in his court.

Kabir (1440-1518), a master Sufi poet and Guru Nanak Dev (1469-1539) the founder of the Sikh religion, were near the age of Akbar although he never met them in person. Akbar knew them rather through their writings, which were read to him by his courtiers. Both Kabir and Nanak Dev wished to eradicate Hindu and Muslim antagonism by uniting the two communities at the spiritual level. They condemned polytheism and insisted that there existed a "divine oneness" (*Tawhid-i-Illahi*). They also decried the caste system, which they found to be immoral and destructive. But, while Kabir subscribed to the doctrine of the transmigration of souls, Kabir did not and pundits of both philosophies found cause to argue for years concerning these issues.[40]

Although different in the particulars of their teachings, upon their respective deaths these two great saints received an unusual tribute. Both Hindus and Muslims claimed them as their own and their words are studied today in both traditions.[41] The essential teaching that affected Akbar was their unified call to people for freedom from formalism. They claimed that whatever name one decided to call God, the differences were artificial, as God belonged to all above distinctions and differences. Both groups of Bhaktis and Sufis were trying to spread these ideas among the larger constituencies of Muslims and Hindus. These two particular ecstatic and mystical groups, supported by the brilliant poetry and inspired writings of their master teachers, were attempting to loosen up a long historic

---

[39] The root of Sufism cannot be known. Some Sufi teachings say that the beginnings of Truth and Wisdom and the origins and return of wisdom will continue to go on after the annihilation of the body. The purity of Truth and Wisdom are everywhere and in all things and the Sufis are humble companions of these ideals. D Some Sufi teachings say that the essence of Truth and Wisdom is everywhere and in all things, and will live on after the annihilation of the body.
[40] Burke, 1989, P.95.
[41] Ibid. P. 95

stronghold of fixated thinking. They were both forging a middle path that would be acceptable to both religions.

Since the Mogul Emperors historically were Hanafis by persuasion,[42] the presumption that the Emperor was Hanafi inclined gave the Muslim *'ulama* the appearance of being the religious leaders of the land. Historically, they usually assumed priority positions in the Mogul court. The Emperor was expected to follow ethical guidelines (*Shari'ah*) and rule his people in accordance with Islamic law. If the Emperor contravened the *Shari'ah*, a *fatwa* (a religious or judicial pronouncement) would be issued and a powerful leader could oust the Emperor learned in Islamic law (*Alim*)[43]. Akbar was under continued pressure by the *Alim* and because he favored open discussion in his courtly gatherings, many orthodox members misunderstood Akbar's motivation for fairness and rather saw his efforts as countering Islamic doctrine.

One of the most powerful *Alim* living in Akbar's time was Mulla Abdul Qadir Badaoni (1540-1615). He was an orthodox Sunni and was a famous historian of the Sunni party during Akbar's reign. He was also a translator of the Indian languages and dialects to Persian. He wrote an important abstract of histories of the Muslim Kings of India with special attention to Akbar's reign, entitled <u>Muntakhabut Tawarikh.</u> His book reflects his orthodox perspective, which contradicted Akbar's philosophical ideas. He believed Akbar destroyed the Islamic religion in India because he encouraged tolerance of other faiths by advancing his ideas of Peace with All (*sulk-i-kul*)[44] instead of teaching the precepts of Islam. Badaoni extended his hatred to Sufis and Shias alike and especially

---

[42] al-Faruqi and Sopher, 1963. P. 262. The Hanifiyyah (tradition of the Hanifs) were considered thoroughbred Arabs and members of their tribes in good standing. Neither Jewish nor Christian in faith, they rejected association with any of the cults prevalent in pre-Islamic Arabia. They professed adherence to the faith of Abraham, Noah, and the early prophets of the Semitic peoples and they were monotheists and ethically motivated Universalists. They assimilated Sumerian, Babylonian, Noahic, Abrahamic and Mosaic religious traditions as well as Rabbinic and Pauline tenets. With the advent of Islam the re-crystallization of the Semitic vision took a radical turn through the founder and proponent of the Hanafi School, Nu'man ibn Thabit, Abu Hanifah, (b.80 A.H.), who felt Islam would be the religion for all men. Abu Hanifah believed the sources of Islamic law are the Qur'an, and the *sunnah* (precedents of the Prophet). His teaching quickly became an established tradition.
[43] "*Alim*" is singular for " *'ulama.*"
[44] Alam Khan, 1999, P. 231, also termed *Sulk-i-kul*, meaning "absolute peace," as well as "peace with all," and "universal brotherhood." Srivastrava, 1998. P.162.

despised the teachings of Kabir and Guru Nanak Dev. He showed little respect for Akbar's faithful historian, Abul Fazl and regarded him as an officious sycophant. Although there is some truth in Badaoni's opinion about Abul Fazl, the main reason why Akbar held Abul Fazl in such high regard was due to his freedom from religious bias and his Sufi outlook, which concurred with Akbar's basic inclination.[45]

Abul Fazl wrote an inscription for a temple in Kashmir that expresses his personal philosophy:

> "If it be a mosque, people murmur the holy prayer, and if it be a Christian church, people ring the bell from love to Thee. Sometimes I frequent the Christian cloister, and sometimes the mosque, but it is Thou whom I search from temple to temple."[46]

Abul Fazl disapproved of bloodshed and was willing to explore any possibility that would prevent hostilities from arising. It was probably for Abul Fazl's fairness and temperate disposition that Badaoni despised him so intensely. Badaoni was a fiery orthodox cleric and a passionate orator. He wanted Akbar to be guided by the conservative *'ulama*, but the presence of Abul Fazl and the Sufis gave Akbar the needed wall of support for an effective counterpoise to the orthodox perspective. Akbar was setting new trends and his originality was beginning to take firm hold in his court and the empire. Yes, Badaoni was right in one basic fact. Akbar was moving away from the religion of his birth but he was walking closer to the true path of the Prophet Mohammed (SAAwS). This was shown in the universality evident in the Prophet's mission to befriend other who believed in God but practiced a different faith than that of Islam. The Prophet's mission says that one lives and establishes Islam on the basis of rationalism as one applies interpretative work (*ijtihad*) to all laws and imperatives set down in *Shari'ah*.[47] It seemed to Akbar that those who opposed the rational freethinking approach put

---

[45] Burke, 1989. P.101.
[46] Ibid. P.102
[47] The renown Muslim scholar, Sheikh Muhammad Rashid Rida confirms the Prophets mission of Islam in his interpretation of Surah Al-Ma'idah. Al-Ghazzali, Muhammad. The Thematic Commentary of the Qur'an. London: International Institute of Islamic Thought, 2000. P.103.

themselves in opposition to God and completely undermined the essence of the *Shari'ah* of Islam and its relevance and effect.

Badaoni was also correct in his declaration that Akbar favored the Shia' over the Sunnis. It is very clear, however, that though Akbar might have approved of certain mystical ideas of the Shia' as against orthodox Sunni tenets, the recorded court documents[48] do not indicate that he was either in favor of the Shia sect or against the Sunni. His examination of doctrines was impartial with reference to both sects and he questioned the basis of both, probing into the private life and sayings of the Prophet Mohammad (*Hadith, Hadith Qudsi*) to anchor his understanding. The Prophet's actions and words were filled with moral choices and set a precedent for the people of his age. Akbar spent hours examining the moral behavior of his wife Ayesha. He questioned the possibilities of miracles attributed to the Prophet, and disapproved of the idea of Paradise and Hell. Akbar rejected many fundamental doctrines that were common to both sects. Badaoni might have been confused and threatened by Akbar's favoritism toward the Shia perspective, particularly when Akbar was in agreement with the Sufis rather than with Sunni doctrine. Badaoni was hyper-sensitive especially when the tenets of the Sunni sect could not be successfully maintained such as daily prayer protocol by its protagonist. The vigorous onslaught of opponents who stood with Akbar turned into a philosophical impasse between the two men. Akbar agreed at various times with the Shia's, the Christians, Hindus, or Jains. But Badaoni believed that Akbar's motivation to side with any opponent of the Sunni sect was to bring the Sunni's discomfiture.[49] Although Badaoni was considered a valuable historian of Akbar's reign, he had an obvious 'ax to grind' regarding the Emperor's visionary experiments. His contrary perspective is found in all his writings and serves as a balance to Abul Fazl's unerring support and love of his King.

Badaoni held blame for three persons' influence over Akbar whom he believed turned him against the tenets of Islam. Of course, Abul Fazl was Badaoni's major target, along with Hakim Abul Fath and Birbal, all devoted members of Akbar's inner circle. They

---

[48] Court documents are recorded in the AkbarNama by Abul Fazl, Vols. I, II, and III.
[49] Krishnamurti, 1961. P.90

possessed great intellectual wit and were known to uplift Akbar's serious disposition. The three men supported a policy for tolerance (*sulk-i-kul*) and under-girded Akbar's efforts to build greater dialogue among the pundits of the many faith systems that found representation in his court. Birbal, the only Hindu in Akbar's inner circle, rose to the ranks of Raja although he came from a poor Hindu class. He supported Akbar's Zoroastrian practices and worship of the sun, and even composed a hundred different words for the sun that Akbar recited every morning. Birbal was against the killing of animals and preferred to worship them as well as the elemental forms of existence that were honored in his prayers and poetry. Akbar and Birbal adored one another. Their relationship was deeply soulful and they remained close companions throughout their lives.

CHAPTER 8

Manhood

As Akbar entered the stages of spiritual awakening in his early twenties his concern for those people in his Empire living in less fortunate circumstances was pressing on his conscience. His love of animals was ever foremost in his heart, particularly his elephants and tigers, and he began establishing laws that protected them. Akbar abolished the practice of enslaving the families of defeated enemies when he was twenty (1562), and abolished the pilgrim tax the next year and the *jizya* the following year (1564).[50] These taxes were traditionally levied against followers of other religious persuasions than that of the conqueror. He also conciliated the Rajputs by marrying their princesses starting when he was twenty, and he continued to appoint Hindus to high office, offering them major responsibility in his empire.

In August 1573, at the age of thirty-one, when he set out to quell the rebellion in Gujarat, a battle which we will discus shortly, the majority of the senior officers in his entourage were Hindus.[51] This marked a monumental shift in a Mogul court one that set the standard of integration for years to follow.

Though Akbar was still in his early years of manhood, he was beginning to lay the foundation of a secular nation-state in India. He wanted to separate religion from politics due to the disparity and flagrant breach of ethics he found among all of the religious orders and faith systems. This strongly motivated him to reject the Islamic theory of religious dominance of the state and declare himself the national monarch of India. Some historians state that he wanted to take this role to aggrandize himself simply because he had the power to do so. But other historians disagree with this assessment of his

---

[50] The reasons for the abolition of these taxes are striking. With regard to the Pilgrim tax, Akbar often said that to demand money from the Hindu pilgrims was tantamount to placing a stumbling block in the way of what they considered a means of worshipping the Creator. This perspective was in sharp contrast to the previous Muslim rulers who imposed the *jizya* out of enmity. Some Muslim writers justify the levy of the *jizya* on the Hindus as the price for their exemption from military service but it was a discriminatory tax all the same and its abolition was an important step towards placing the Hindus on the same level of citizenship as the Muslims. Akbar abolished the *jizya* in spite of the disapproval of statesmen and of the loss of great revenue.
[51] Burke, 1989, P.110

motivation. For them, his primary goal was to raise the policy of religious toleration to the pinnacle of secularism and from there promote the spiritual ideal of monotheism and ethical teachings which were free of priest craft among Hindus and Muslims. This he could do by eliminating all the racial, religious and cultural barriers between adherents of the two faiths.[52]

With orthodox Islamic pundits building opposition against him, it was necessary that Akbar develop an effective ploy for preventing the *'ulama* from misusing their religious powers to become politically dominant or cause divisiveness in his empire. After isolating himself for days in contemplation, he decided he would assume the spiritual position of counsel for the multi-religious and multi-cultural subjects who were being protected in his empire. He had only to find a way to take this new position by earning the respect of the religious representatives. He finally found cause to break his long-standing rebellion, and learned to present—probably by memorization—the sermon or oration (*khutbah*) delivered on Fridays at the time of *zuhr*, or median prayer in the mosque as well as leading the opening prayer of Qur'an (*Fatiha*) for the congregation. This was a new step never before claimed by any Emperor before him, and his recitations soon won him the Islamic pundits' support. Akbar then began a bold and strategic shift toward his goal of placing the foundations of tolerance, (*sulk-i-kul*) "Peace with All," in his Empire.

As Akbar moved forward toward his religious experiment of *sulk-i-kul*, he fell backwards into deep melancholy. Unresolved issues from his past pulled him ever more strongly into his addiction of drugs and drunkenness. His chemically induced rages churning the unbalanced aspects of his personality would blacken his conscience and mark his efforts for the rest of his life, bringing unforeseen difficulties and doubt to his legacy in later years.

Repeating an obsessive pattern, his insatiable libido burst out of control and he began to focus on the possession of another princess from the court of Rana Uday Singh's harem.

---

[52] Srivastava, 1998, P.159.

When it came to sexual desire, he demanded immediate gratification, and if refused he became like a monster insanely possessed. Frustrated and out of control at Uday Singh's refusal to allow Akbar access to his harem in Chitor, Akbar's rage built like a fuming volcano. He decided to wage a most brutal war on Chitor, a staunch Hindu community that disapproved of Mogul rule and was considered a Rajput stronghold. Also, Chitor was a constant irritant to Akbar's sovereignty as they refused to recognize him. That they held their Rajput independence up to the 15th Century of Mogul rule galled Akbar and gave him multiple excuses to obliterate the community completely.

The brutality that Akbar exhibited in his wrath was like no other military strike he had made before. He gathered his huge army around him and slaughtered with his sword anyone who was in his way as he screamed the name of God wildly (*Allah hu Akbar*).[53] After raging on in this killing madness for nine straight hours, finally exhausted, he had his generals return to Chitor and slaughter anything, human or creature, that was left living. Almost every man, woman and child in the community of Chitor was annihilated. His order even gave his army permission to plunder, breaking his ethic of noble conquest which he had upheld so fervently. This terrible siege brought the Rajput community to near extinction. The atrocities that the imperial army committed were horrifying, in fact people would literally vomit upon hearing the details.

Chitor fell to the Mogul army in 1586 when Akbar was twenty-six years old. Little did Akbar know at the time how his action in Chitor would set the stage for unexpected betrayal years later. Indeed this siege would come to haunt him many times through his life, because such unconscious actions influenced by opiates set in motion cycles of patterning that his sons would emulate later in their reigns.

During the siege of Chitor, an extraordinary event did serve to curb Akbar's ferocious madness, the intervention of a fourteen-year-old Rajput girl named Mira who managed to escape the slaughter. Unafraid of his exacerbated wildness she stood before Akbar in guileless purity and asked him to put his sword away and interceded for what remnants

---

[3] *Allah hu Akbar*, meaning God is great or/even beyond any conception of greatness.

were left of her extinguished community. Akbar's his rage was immediately quelled by her appeal and he fell into a passive swoon. He favored Mira in his harem for many years to follow for she had an unusually soothing power over him.

Women impressed Akbar greatly. He was intrigued and enchanted by them not only because they satisfied his voracious libidinal drive but because he always found them to be generous and self-sacrificing. He worshipped beauty and he felt that women were closer to the Creator because they were more beautiful in form, face and manner. He loved being surrounded by his harem, which numbered in the thousands and was the most exquisite collection of beauties that one could ever imagine together in one place.

There was only one woman, Rani Durgawati, who entirely perplexed Akbar. She was the heroine Queen of Gondwana, located in the northern area of Madhya Pradesh. She was a warrior Queen who led her armies numbering seventy thousand men, to victory. She was famous throughout the neighboring districts because she rode her great elephants and wore full battle armor. She knew all the surrounding chieftains and effectively cultivated an immediate method for conflict resolution. She was worshipped as a Goddess and related to all men with fierce strength and truthfulness.

Warriors and chieftains such as Baz Bahador and the Tajik warrior Asof Khan attempted to defeat her in battle but she was too fast and clever, often out-witting them through her skillful military strategies. Her army was so devoted to her that they often exuded miraculous powers in battle. Her end also was extraordinary. When her son Raja Bir Narayan was wounded in battle with Asof Khan, she ran into the middle of the field pick him up and was wounded in the neck by an arrow during the rescue attempt. She bravely pulled the arrow out with her own strength. After swooning from the extreme pain, she took out a dagger and struck a blow to her own heart so that her army would not endure the shame of seeing her captured.

The glory of womanhood modeled in the warrior Queen's life exerted an enduring power on the extended community where Rani Durgawati held her court. Akbar was drawn to ontemplate why a Queen would choose such a difficult life of a warrior over that of gentle and passive beauty. But he never understood women of unique powers and maintained a parochial attitude regarding the opposite sex for his entire life making matters of courtly harmony between men and women incredibly difficult for him.

At this period in Akbar's life, one prominent dilemma surfaced rapidly. Peace, the longing desire of his soul that the Sufis had watered, was a paradox for him because at this time in his life he understood peacefulness as a repugnant, stagnant state unfitting for a military man. Peace as a welcome calm in the storm, a state that reflected freedom from disquieting and oppressive thoughts and conditions within and without his turbulent psyche, seemed unreachable. How could Akbar believe in the benefits of a tranquil state when he was intent on expanding his powers and meeting contentious and troublesome forces standing against him?

However, while Akbar was not yet able to work out the implementation of these ideals the salient strategy of *sulk-i-kul* was taking form in the far recesses of his being. He was driven to follow his father's modeling as a dominating expansionist while unconsciously reinterpreting the ferocious, conquering Mogul archetype of his genetic ancestry. He did not realize that he was going to lay this archetype down and replace it with a new ideal of his own making.

By this time in his life he had acquired the territories of Samurkand, Qandhar, Bokhara, Badakhshan, Farghana and Kabul. He loved Hindustan and he considered Agra his true home. Delhi and the Punjab were in his hands, and the regions across the Khyber never entered his mind.[54] Still blind to the repercussions of his Mogul modeling to dominate and conquer, he decided to turn his energy toward developing popular support among his people. He began to build a firm identification with the conditions that needed improvement where he felt his leadership could effectively have an impact, such as in architecture, education, and enhancement of the arts and sciences.

---

[54] Lal, 1980. P. 124.

As Akbar's love and concern for Hindustan grew, he still held hatred for the Rajput spirit of independence and they in turn despised his Mogul influence and suzerainty. The Rajputs saw the Muslim nobility as being drawn from groups with unresolved tribal conflicts—Turks, Tartars, Persians, Indians and Afghans—that were a constant cause of political instability. Akbar needed the Rajputs support to firm up the territorial boundary to his empire and they despised him and resisted him. To show Akbar how much the Rajputs hated him, when news reached them that Akbar was waging an attack on Chitor, the court women numbering 1300 set themselves on fire rather than being taken into his harem. The smoking pyres of another group of female corpses were shocking to Akbar, causing him to back up into deep inner reflection once again.

He decided that a second pilgrimage to the Dargah of the Sufi Saint, Khwaja Moineddin Chisthi in Ajmer was necessary. As before, he walked most of the journey on foot but this time he was distracted by his thousands of harem women and courtly entourage who, out of courtesy, were accompanying and walking behind him. Their continued complaints and hardships caused him to interrupt his journey frequently so he decided to send for palanquins to carry the members of the procession, while he distanced himself from the group for his pilgrimage.

Akbar walked much of the way as penitence for his actions at Chitor, which was heavily weighing upon his conscience throughout the journey. Out of remorse and guilt he gave away golden coins to everyone he met in the many villages he passed through. Robes of honor were given to Imams as well as bestowal of courtly privileges to common citizens. Akbar felt that each gift given was a stain washed away from the killings he committed at Chitor.

After reciting prayers and maintaining deep contemplation (*khilvat*), he began feeling more relieved of the burden of guilt. He began to rationalize his military aggression at Chitor as a Divine mission given to him by God. He knew he needed to control the territory for his empire's safety. Destroying the Rajput's community and the leaders who refused to join his vision of inter-communal support of his empire was acceptable to

Akbar's military strategy. This was the beginning of his realization that he might be the true Divine agent on earth (*Mahdi*). He somehow knew he was on his way to fulfilling the prediction at his birth by his astrologers but he had not yet found the method that gave their prediction the form that would solidify his mission. Several years later, Akbar spoke these words to the Portuguese Jesuit Missionary Aquaviva:

> "Kings cannot be saints, or saints kings, each has its own place in the scheme of life. It is best that they continue to perform their assigned duties. Maybe at some future date, the saint-king concepts of the ancient Hindus may come to be realized. It is a distant dream, an ideal that must forever, like a mirage, continue to allure the credulous. I am not a stargazer; neither am I a searcher after things that do not appear to exist. Each man has a mission to perform. Mine is to unite this great land. The sword has a definite role to play in this assignment. Even God has sanctioned the use of force....."[55]

In his depths, Akbar felt he was an instrument for the divine conversion of his people. He was first and foremost a military man who aimed to expand his territory. Yet his desire to unite Hindustan under his liberal direction was strong. Assured of his destiny during this pilgrimage to Khwaja Moineddin Chisthi's Dargah, he decided to build the famous city Fatehpur Sikri. His dream-city, which was to commemorate his Empire, would be a place where he would begin his spiritual work[56] of installing the principles of a Divine Religion (*Din-i-Illahi*) through methods of tolerance and peace with all (*sulk-i-kul*).

For seventeen years in a row, throughout Akbar's early and middle years he attended the Urs celebration of Khwaja Moineddin Chisthi, a special ritual event commemorating his death. He would also make many pilgrimages at other times so that he could sit in the presence of this great Sufi Saint of Ajmer for his own heart's contemplation. He felt so dedicated to his pilgrimage because he was always inspired in the atmosphere of the Saints tomb, and it was not until he shifted his capital to Lahore in the later part of his life

---

[55] Ibid. P.142,143. Akbar felt justified in his understanding of battle as the Prophet Mohammed used a sword when it was necessary toward fulfilling the purpose of greater unity.
[56] Ibid. P.133

that he stopped going to Ajmer. These moments of inspiration became intrinsic to Akbar who firmly believed that the spiritual powers of the living and the dead men of God influenced the affairs of the world[57]. He upheld this belief for the whole of his life.

Following his pilgrimages, he gave evidence to the inspirations received at the Saint's Dargah through his generosity. His main gift of charity was to offer various boons to the needy members of the community bringing them up to higher levels of community function. He tried to remain reverent to Sufi principles and methods to help his fellow human beings gain respect for themselves. Akbar gleaned the tools necessary to bring the Sufi principles of recognizing the Divine in all beings into direct application. He saw the Sufis as guides in living with charity, wisdom, and unity within his empire. His manner clearly stood in opposition to the quarrelsome religious pundits whose preaching only brought further dissent and separation among the people.

With the Rajputs still holding grievous wounds from Akbar's atrocities at Chitor, a dead hero of Chitor, Jai Mal's son Raja Bihari Mal was now in a position to wreck vengeance in a most unexpected way that would affect Akbar in his mature years. Raja Bihari Mal's daughter, Jodha Bai, Akbar's trusted harem wife of many years, became pregnant and gave birth to his first son whom he named Salim. He was to become the future Emperor (Jahangir) after Akbar's death and Jodha Bai was to become the Queen of Prayers (*Malika-i-Muezamma*), with all powers and influence enjoyed by the mother of the heir-apparent (*Wali-Ahad*). The birth of Akbar's son Salim at Fatehpur Sikri brought sheer joy to Akbar. The mother was blessed for giving Akbar a prized son and Salim received profound blessings as he was named after the Sufi Sheikh Salim Chisthi.

Salim's birth enlivened the court and great celebrations followed for both mother and child, and Jodha Bai's value as one of his true and trusted confidants and a pivotal player in the affairs of courtly life became more precious to Akbar. As their relationship was refining into mutual respect, Akbar had no idea what disappointments and challenges lay

---

[57] Ibid. P.172

ahead between Salim and himself as well as the brewing difficulties caused by Jodhi Bai's father.

Akbar wanted Jodha Bai and Salim to live in the environment of Sheikh Salim Chisthi's benediction and prepared magnificent accommodations for them at Fatepur Sikri which was situated very close to Sheikh Salim's old quarters. Any of his wives who would become pregnant were asked to come to the beautiful and holy palace that was luxuriously redesigned by Akbar and his team of master craftsmen. Bibi Salima Begum gave birth to Akbar's first daughter, named Khanum, on Nov. 21st 1569. Soon after Salima Sultan Begum, widow of Bairam Khan, whom Akbar married in 1561, gave birth to his second son, Murad Shah on June 7th 1570. Two more daughters, Shukr-un-Nisa and Aram Banu Begam were born before his third son Daniyal, was born in Ajmer in 1572.[58]

Akbar was now somewhat settled knowing he had two royal bred sons as successors, Salim and Murad as well as Daniyal, born of a concubine, and other children who would preserve his legacy. But he could not overcome the dominating imprint of his father's warrior archetype nor alter his verve to push on to battle once again. He felt that his military initiative for greater expansion would protect the empire he was building. His dynastic legacy now in place, he moved with a feeling of certainty about his future. He was determined to leave a large amount of territory to his successors so that the Timirid Empire would remain unchallenged by peripheral forces. At this time in his life, his primary focus was on external problems but he had yet to consider those difficulties arising from within his own Empire, his court and eventually his own sons.

---

[58] Ibid. P.161

CHAPTER 9

Gujarat

Contented and secure in the domination of land around his Empire, Akbar began to turn to his people and examine the needs of cultural and religious cross-fertilization. He focused first on architecture and beauty. But although his years at Fatehpur Sikri were more placid this endeavor did not help him arrive at ease. While he had conquered the central and northern portions of India he began to worry about the conditions in the South and the East. He knew that his father Humayun had held Gujarat for a time but it had swayed from Akbar's rule under the influence of the prominent local chiefs. The four Mirzas – Ibrahim Hussain, Shah Hussain, Muhammad Hussain and Masud Hussain – were gaining military strength and rebelling against Akbar's imperial governance. Unable to tolerate this threat, Akbar mobilized an attack on July 4th, 1572 to lead a victorious army into Ahmadabad, the capital of Gujarat and capture the city once again. Attempting to stand against Akbar's imperial forces in Ujjain, the quartet took refuge in Gujarat and carved out a semi-independent kingdom.[59]

Abul Fazl mentions in his coverage of the quick conquest of Gujarat that Akbar always inquired into and sympathized with the condition of the oppressed. Hence wherever the rulers acted wisely and exerted themselves to protect their subjects, he did not attempt to conquer that country.[60] Akbar felt the Mirzas were not concerned about the needs of the people and caring for others was beginning to dawn on Akbar's heart as the purest motivation of a King.

Although feeling morally justified in his reasoning to challenge the four Mirzas, Akbar's drive for expansion was the central motive that led him to this battle. It was his most ferocious killing spree, even surpassing Chitor. Akbar entered a state of unremitting frenzy that caused enemies to shudder at his approach. He appeared invincible with a

---

[59] Ibid, P. 166
[60] Fazl, (Vol II), 1977, P.536

newly unleashed strength that supported his customary disregard of danger. He was ready to kill anything that crossed his path. The opposition fell quickly and Gujarat was in his hands in a matter of hours as the local chiefs fled into the hills after seeing the vast size of the Imperial army.

Akbar's desire for conquest, which gave him successes in the Northwestern and Central territory of India, now caused him to finally gaze to the East where Cambay opened to the sea. There the vast ocean lay before him, which he saw for the first time in his life. The moment his eyes saw the oceanic vista he was entranced and the sea became a symbol of the infinite largess of God, an impression he held in his heart till the end of his days.

The Mirzas ran and the King of Gujarat surrendered easily. Akbar returned to Fatephur Sikri with a burning desire to begin his real work. To commemorate his victory he renamed Sikri as Fatehabad, which by common usage became Fatehpur.[61] However, he was not to stay long as the Mirzas had assembled forces to turn against Akbar for a second time. He headed back in record time with a larger army than before, and soon the severed heads of the Mirzas were in his hands. Like his father and his grandfather before him, he once again built a pyramid of bodies of the slaughtered in the battlefield to mark his victory and stultify any further rebellion. His plan worked and Gujarat was solidly in his hands.

---

[61] Burke, 1989, P.193

CHAPTER 10

Akbar's Mission to Bengal

The sea viewed from Cambay invigorated Akbar and he wanted to expand his Empire once again and lay claim to land across the seas. He felt the future of his empire would be safer if the entry to his vast territorial holdings particularly from the sea was guarded and protected by his Imperial forces. Most of the Northwestern and Central regions of India were now under his sway. Bengal was beautiful, wealthy in resources, tropical and green. As seductive as the land was, epidemics and radical weather patterns occurred on a regular basis. But this land provided a sensuous air and hospitality that Akbar loved and again a ravenous desire arose that drove him to sail to the distant land of Patna in his verve for expansion and conquest.

Akbar regarded these surges of conquest and war as a Divine worship and a means to realization of the highest Divine law (*Dharma*) by an Emperor. He commissioned two huge ships to be built upon his design so that his favorite elephants, Bal Sundar and Suman could fit comfortably in them. He made spacious quarters for his whole entourage, which numbered in the thousands and the crafts were veritable floating palaces.

He left Cambay in the most unfavorable circumstances and against his counselor's advice. The winds and rains were tumultuous and the sea was heaving enormous waves. Even with these conditions Akbar set sail and he enjoyed as no other the challenge of meeting the storm. He loaded the harem women, the mothers of the young children, the princes and princesses on board. The journey was horrendously disagreeable for the courtly party but exhilarating for Akbar. He directed the main army to cross the northern terrain and meet him in Patna.

It was during one night out on a calm sea, when he was enjoying the full group of Qawali singers he had invited to join his entourage, that a strange state overtook Akbar. The group began to sing a composition in praise and dedication to the Holy Prophet Mohammed (*SAAwS*). He began to swoon and move into a deep emotional state that made him weep uncontrollably. He removed himself quickly to his own quarters to be alone and to contemplate the experience. After being shut away for a few days, he requested of the Qawali singers that the same song be sung every night. The singers became embodiments of his spiritual longing throughout the seafaring journey, and he rewarded them lavishly with gold and rare food delicacies and all comforts imaginable.

Akbar's complex nature is striking. He was a man of sensuality and uncontrolled violence and yet he could cry at a beautiful song. He could find great peacefulness in the presence of the young girl, Mira, who rendered him pliable and harmless after the violent siege in Chitor. This tenderness in his personality that he unabashedly revealed to members of his court without constraint often gave the impression to others that he was indeed a sensitive spiritual leader (*Mahdi*) of his people as well as the Padshah and military genius of his Empire. This impression amongst his entourage of a multifaceted personality existing in one human being was seminal to the confirmation of his vision of tolerance in his new religion (*Din-i-Illahi*). He could perceive two diverse aspects of his personality living in harmony in his own heart and this is what the Sufis teachings brought into reconciliation. He knew when he returned to the embattled issues with the '*ulama* in Fatehpur Sikri that his self-reliance would be solid, for it was now based on an integrated spiritual and emotional unification.

Even when the storms grew fiercer, sinking one flotilla, Akbar moved with certainty that Divine purpose infused his every move and he regarded nature as his advocate not his adversary. When he stopped at Allahabad and Benares to find out news about Shah Daud Khan's encampment and learn about the prepared threat against his Imperial army he was confirmed in his Divine fiat to succeed above all costs. Daud was a young, handsome and tactless fellow who mistakenly thought it ambitious to provoke Akbar through increasing bellicosity and flamboyant gestures that dishonored Akbar's imperial sovereignty. Akbar's army was enormous compared to the small battalion of fighters gathered together by the frivolous son of an aging, and pessimistic Afghan king. Understanding the great inequity of the battle and certain of his success, Akbar sent a letter to Daud saying:

> "In a few days we shall be at the gates of Patna. Beware of the danger that lies ahead of you and your besieged men. We are resolved to crush all opposition to our arms. However, to save bloodshed, I make an offer that we decide the fate of the territories now under your nominal control through a dual. The choices of weapons are left to you. In case you do not find yourself equal to accepting this generous offer, may I suggest that the issue be decided by duel between our chosen proxies. Even if this is not acceptable, I am prepared to take all on a fight between our two elephants. In making these sporting offers, we are motivated by human considerations, and these alone. Wars, though necessary, are not unavoidable. We hope you will see the writing on the wall, and surrender unconditionally. You may depend upon our generosity for a fair deal to you, your family, your officers and your men."[62]

As the rain poured down in monsoon fashion, breaking the banks of the Jamuna and Ganga, Daud turned down Akbar's offer to surrender. A siege was waged under the most untenable weather conditions as Daud set in motion three thousand soldiers against Akbar's tens of thousands. Daud quickly fled and Akbar pursued, but he escaped Akbar's capture by traveling over mountainous terrain into inaccessible regions of Bengal. As Akbar waited for other opportunities to capture Daud, he fed his intellectual inquisitiveness, sharpened his spiritual ideas and sought spiritual knowledge by talking to many Holy men. As moisture borne diseases and homesickness were ravaging Akbar's army, he made an unexpected acquaintance with another form of belief.

During his encampment in Bengal Akbar met with the Portuguese Christians. He wanted good relations with them because he had to pass through their territory with his harem on pilgrimage to Mecca. Portuguese dignitaries had previously visited him on his earlier

---

[62] Lal, 1980, P. 190

passage from Surat to Ahmedabad. He was familiar with their religious protocol such as their manner of greeting and proper dress. In deference and respect Akbar often wore the Portuguese costume and allowed dignitaries to kiss his hand but he had never spoken at length with the Christian missionaries. He was very impressed when he learned about a certain Jesuit priest who had refused a Christian merchant absolution because he had defrauded the Mogul government of taxes due.[63]

This kind of ethical behavior impressed Akbar greatly as the incident convinced him that Christian principles, which condemned dishonesty, even when practiced against an alien government, must possess exceptional value and influence over the hearts of men.[64] He also inquired into Christianity with the ambassador to the emperor at Surat Antonio Cabral, who was sent to Bengal by the Viceroy of Goa. Through his introduction to Christian doctrine missionaries from Goa were dispatched to Fatephur Sikri and the profoundly influential association with Father Monserrate began to develop
With the introduction to the Jesuits established, yet not finding closure with the capture of Daud, Akbar left Bengal and returned to Fatephur Sikri. The capture of Shah Daud Khan came after many months of political intrigues with allies favorable to the Mogul Imperial throne. After Daud surfaced and disappeared again trying to regain his empire, his severed head was finally brought before Akbar. This final conquest brought to an end all surrounding opposition as well as the lineage of independent Afghan kings in Bengal.

In 1581, at thirty-nine years old, Akbar entered a grand turning point in his life. Contented with his success in Bengal, which assured him of safety at the peripheral borders, Akbar returned to his first and foremost aspiration, which was to continue high quest for knowledge. He immersed himself in his spiritual labors and he would often fall into long nostalgic periods remembering those feelings of unity (*tawhid*) that the Sufis had so deeply impressed upon his heart. He longed for those experiences as he began to envision the future needs of his empire. The review and reevaluation begun when he first started building Fatephur Sikri in 1573 was now fully upon his consciousness.

---

[53] Krishnamurti, 1961.P. 42
[54] Smith, 1958, P.97.

He realized, during his exchange of spiritual dialogue with the learned men in his court, that he was able to dive deeply into the gems of mystical expression, and he yearned to translate them into action. Although his ideal was set, his method was uncertain, but this did not impede his unflinching impetus to begin a new era.

CHAPTER 11

The Din-i-Illahi at Fatepur Sikri

As Akbar recounted his original dream and gazed back into the past, he recognized that it was in September 1573 when he was 31 years old that his dream of Fatehpur Sikri had began. He resolved then to craft his architectural designs for building a magnificent city of beauty and balance and to deepen his spiritual quest. He wanted to construct a city of gratitude dedicated to Sheikh Salim Chisthi who had settled in the rocks nearby as a hermit in 1537-8 and had constructed an old monastery and schoolhouse in the area. Akbar's gratitude for the Sheikh's blessings for the birth of his heirs to the empire was evident in the care he took in the design. The city was composed of beautiful palaces, gardens, schools, colleges, houses for the grandees of the empire, mosques, playgrounds, libraries, court rooms, roads, public parks and lakes. It took Akbar, and the many thousands of laborers and master artisans almost fourteen years to complete his vision.

During the long hours that Akbar worked with the planners for Fatehpur Sikri, he made a point to freely allot houses to those workers who wished to establish a home within the city. Akbar wanted to encourage people to build houses with his blessings, so long as they followed the symmetry of the cohesive civic plan, so that the barren land would be filled with beauty and splendor.

As stated in the _Tarikh-i-Akbari_,

> "In 1576 an imperial order was issued that from the court up to the gate, which faces the capital city's beautiful shops of red stone with lime, plaster houses may be built. Moreover, four bazaars well designed and decorated were also built near it... Beside the said monuments which should be regarded as the model of exceptional engineering skill of the emperor, there is a blessed palace which is the guardian of the house of the state and its dignity, and on account of which nine

skies seem to be ashamed and amazed and which has the height of the sky and its ornamentation…

…In the courtyard of this high edifice, which touches the sky, beginning from one side four chambers, four raised platforms and four halls have been made so skillfully that the watchmen of all the eight paradises feel staggered with wonderment. Royal houses and government offices have been built around it. In the center of the courtyard a tank is laid and its water is considered the blessing of the early dawn. The reflection of man's face can be seen very clearly in it, which excels the mirror called *Jahan Numa*. One can see each particle of sand up to its depths, which can be counted and even the eggs of the fish can be seen. This pond is like a river; not that it is a river without head or tail. In 1578 the pond was emptied of its water and in its place it was filled up with copper, silver and gold coins (*tankas*) in such a way that intelligence was helpless in sounding its depth, nor the imagination of travelers could see its banks."[65]

There was no end to the lavishness that Akbar envisioned and manifested. Magnificently designed houses were built for Abul Fazl and his brother Faizee and other members of his inner circle giving all whose eyes fell upon the grand structures an image of the Emperor's pleasure. Intricate frescoed designs decorated the buildings bringing integrity and strength to the central part of the community as Akbar's way of offering gratitude and royal patronage to those who helped him in the transformation of his ideals as an Emperor.

The emphasis on architectural beauty and integrity gave Akbar the feelings of accomplishment that were fundamental to his laying out his spiritual ideals. Beauty was a Divine quality upheld and honored by Sufis as it became the correlative expression for the Divine Essence in all things showing forth in nature. With the assistance of two great scholars, Abul Fazl and his brother Faizee, at his side, Akbar was now able to coalesce

---

[65] Qandhari, 1993. Pgs. 185-187. Description of the foundation of Fatehpur Sikri [follows in the construction of Agra as found in the text The Economics and Social Setting-Fatehpur Sikri, edited by Michael Brand and Gleen, D. Lawry, Mary Publications, 1987.

his spiritual message in the "Religion of God" (*Din-i-Illahi*), a synthesis of One message. The purpose of the two faithful brothers work was to build up Akbar's extensive Empire by educating its members in the ethics of tolerance (*sulk-i-kul*) and fairness regarding diverse religious perspectives. These two close companions were gifted with the harmonizing attitudes found in the Sufi teachings from their father Mulla Mubarak and the illustrious school of Sultan-ut-Tarikin Hazrat Khwaja Hameeduddin Nagauri.[66]

The methods used by the two brothers began by developing interaction between Sufism and Hindu traditional thought based on newly translated texts from Sanskrit to Persian notably of the *Mahabharat*,[67] the *Ramayan*[68] and the *Yog Vashishta*[69]. Abul Fazl and Faizee's education in the great classical literature of the age suggested that Gnosticism existed in India before Islam rose as a religious power. This gave validity to Sufi teachings concerning the stations of realization (*makams*) and helped the *'ulama* gain insight into how many non-Muslims could also lead virtuous and religious lives. The Sufis strategy was always considerate and conversion of non-Muslims to Islam was never a deliberate intention for them.[70]

Abul Fazl and Faizee were inspired by the Chisthi Sheikhs like Nizamuddin Auliya who believed that living the example of piety was much more important than following fixed precepts without deeply investigating their meaning. The brothers had no desire to force their brilliant strategies on others or gain acceptance for the model of the "new religion" (*Din-i-Illahi*). They knew as Akbar did, that the ideal of cultural co-existence and true religion was found in the natural order of life, and the unfolding of the heart to the truth that we are One Being living in many forms. This philosophical form of unity was the only living scripture in which one could see God. This idea was in harmony with the

---

[66] Begg, 1956, 1977.P. 169
[67] The Mahabharata (c.500BCE) is the inspiring Hindu epic about the war of the house of Bharata.
[68] The Ramayana (written between c.200BCE and 200CE) consisting of 24,000 couplet tells the tale of Prince Rama and his enforced abdication as royal heir his great struggle with Ravana, and his search for his wife Sita and brother Lakshmana.
[69] Yog Vashistha is considered to be a section of the ancient Rig Veda (c.1200BCE) composed by the leading Vedic Rishi, "Vasishtha" who was a renowned lawgiver.
[70] Alam Khan, 1999. P.33

spirit of the Sufis, particularly that of the Chisthiyya Order, which the brothers and Akbar revered.

Akbar wanted to grant complete religious freedom to his subjects and provide a welcoming spirit of harmony for his people by eliminating the racial, religious and cultural barriers between the various groups. This stance was based on his understanding of Holy Qur'an where the concept of active virtue (*ihsan*) is specifically linked to the concept of Justice (*adl*). The following Iya, (Qur'anic verse) supported his idea "Verily, Allah commands justice (*adl*), the doing of good (*ihsan*), and giving to one's near relatives: He forbids acts of wickedness, vice (*munkar*), and lust (*bagha*)."[71] Akbar also found support for his notion of religious freedom in the references to human rights in other Suras, (chapters) in Holy Qur'an where the concept of justice is expanded to include the notion of epistemological truth. This occurs in a discussion of the ends for which God created the universe: "Not but for just ends (*illa bi-l-haqq*) did Allah create the heavens and the earth and all that is between them."[72] In this verse *al-haqq* not only expresses the idea of truth in an abstract sense, but it also implies the notion of collective and individual rights (*huquq*), as in "human rights" (*huquq al-insan*) or even "divine rights" (*huquq Allah*). Akbar felt that if he could influence the many wise men to study all the Holy Scriptures, these texts would naturally reveal the common elements existing in all the different approaches and assist in bringing his ideal forward.

As Akbar's attention was redirected from the world of politics to the domain of theological concerns it became clear to him that Islam was much more than the observance of ritual practices. He saw the complementarity of faith and practice coinciding with truth and justice. Akbar's own brand of interpretation showing a preference for monotheism was akin to what the *Hanifs* of Mecca and Muhammad himself (*SAAwS*), had practiced. This is why he aligned with the Sufis who were politically active in reforming the term "*ihsan*" to connote the highest degree of Islamic practice which became the model for his pantheistic approach to all other faith systems.

---

[71] Qur'an 16:90
[72] Ibid. 30:8

He now found himself in the middle of a veritable theological college (*madrasa*) setting, with faithful teachers and ardent pupils. He was deeply grieved by the frozen attitudes of the '*ulama* concerning enforced Islamic protocol and although he might have appeared a traitor to the '*ulama*, who considered him to be turning against Muslim orthodoxy, he was ironically following more closely the model of the Holy Prophet's mission (*SAAwS*).

That mission of the Holy Prophet (*SAAwS*) was born from "truth and justice" and the deeper social meaning of "doing good" (*ishan*) to all beings by seeing God in all directions. As is said in Holy Qur'an, "To God belongs the East and the West and whichever way you turn there shall be the face of God. God is Omnipresent and All-Knowing."[73] Akbar's core support undeniably lay in Qur'anic principles, which undeniably were the source from which he took inspiration. He quoted a well known *Iya* (verse): "No three persons talk together in secret without Him being their forth; nor five without Him being their sixth; nor fewer or more, without Him being present with them wherever they may be."[74] Akbar memorized these verses well and he continued to feel longing for a fully integrated society in God's omnipresence. His greatest anxiety came when he found himself surrounded by the institutionalized intolerance from the Muslim leaders. Akbar continued to perceive their rigid religious attitudes and interpretations of scripture as creating fanaticism and separation.

In response to this intolerance, he initiated the practice of holding religious discourses with revered holy leaders and scholars representing the many religions calling them together from all parts of the continent. But his heart was always drawn and illuminated most by his discussions with learned Sufis. After sitting in long conversations with them, he desired to convene a conference to discuss the emergence of the *Mahdi* a religious leader who would recast Islam and reinterpret its tenets in the light of changing circumstances in society. The esoteric mandate of the *Mahdi* was to amend what appeared to be the irreparable damage that was already done by the rigid pundits of Islam who continued to discourage open dialogue and questioning (*itjihad*). The orthodox

---

[73] Ibid. Sura Al-Baqarah, 115
[74] Ibid. Sura Al'Mujadilah, 7

ulama felt that it was not for the different leaders of other religions to declare what the Qur'an stipulated. Also, they said, "Believers must accept what the Qur'an dictates without asking questions about its reason." They held to the tenets that only a revered authority such as an *Alim* or *Imam* could interpret Qur'an for the general populace.

The *'ulama's* resistance among the Sunni and Shia groups took root in the early historic separation that followed the Prophet Muhammad's (*SAAwS*) death when the group surrounding him feuded over who would succeed him, the elder statesmen Abu Bakr or the forth Caliph and son-in-law, Ali. This original argument caused factions to form between the Shia who believed Ali who was the true successor and the Sunni who believed it was Abu Bakr. The antipathy between the groups codified into dogmatic divisions that have remained throughout the centuries. Although both groups follow the ethical laws (*Shari'ah*), including the revealed teachings of Holy Qur'an and the traditional sayings of the Prophet (*Hadiths*), the two groups disagree in matters of lineage and lineage was a serious matter for validation of textual interpretation.

From an orthodox perspective, Muslims had to cultivate an inner sense of understanding. The purity of revelation that defined how one understood the ordinary world verses the Divine realm was essential for self-disclosure to be gained. The Sufis helped in this exchange of ideas concerning inner knowledge, felt anyone could become a Sufi when that person resolved to understand the symbolic meaning hidden in the Holy Scriptures rather than resting in the literal interpretation. The gathering of many religious representatives that Akbar tried to engage in open exchange became perpetually trapped in this unresolved Sunni/Shia issue and could not get to the defining characteristics that united them nor the mystical realms of spiritual unity that called to his being. Akbar's hope for building communication across religious lines was almost frozen except for a brilliant insight offered by Mulla Mubarak.

Mulla Mubarak had forecast that Akbar might be that *Mahdi* which all were awaiting, and told his sons, Abul Fazl and Faizee about his vision. He felt this vision held validity because Akbar refused to be influenced by other leaders around him as he explored the various religious subjects. Akbar did not give in to negativity and intolerance. Mulla Mubarak recognized that Akbar was increasingly concentrated on his subject and in the presence of wise counsel he pursued ideas until he was satisfied with an answer for himself. Sheikh Mubarak, Abul Fazl and Faizee found themselves to be in complete confidence of the Emperor's method of inquiry, as they were not only congenial spiritual companions but held the quest for truth above all dogmatic proclivities.

Because Akbar often pondered and questioned the holy leaders for many hours, holding conversations well into the night, he decided, with the support of his three wise companions, to create a special conference hall for the purpose of spiritual dialogue, which could also serve as a House of Worship. In the *Ibadatkhana* the most prestigious of the Muslims, Hindus, Jains, Sikhs, Sufis, Buddhists, Zoroastrians, and Christians gathered on Thursday and they would enter deliberations going through the night into Friday. According to Abul Fazl, the *Ibadatkhana* was designed with spiritual intention and manifested in its design, with four distinctive verandahs representing the directions from which all religions arise given by the One God.

In the eastern section sat the great leaders and high officers who were conspicuous in the courts of society for their enlightenment. In the southern section, the school of instruction sat the keen sighted investigators, both those who gathered the light of day (i.e. the alumni) and those who chose the repose of the night halls of contemplation. In the western compartment, those of lofty lineage who practiced auspicious arts where placed together. In the northern compartment sat the Sufis of clear heart who were absorbed in beatific visions[75] and considered one of the most important and sacred of tasks. Their pure intention was to protect the gathering from disintegrating into opposition and enmity and above all, to hold the ideal of love and acceptance among the group regardless of differences.

This position in which Akbar placed the Sufis was consonant with the Sufi philosophy of seeing One Divine Presence in All. The Sufis understood that no one is acceptable in

---

[75] Srivastava, 1998, P.167.

God's court except on the basis of love. The lover seeks only love and the realization of this is more important than knowledge itself. The Sufis of 15th century India did not believe in smearing the body with ashes or sitting long hours in meditation; there was no point in wandering naked in the wilderness to find this love. There was no use in fasting or performing prayer remembrance (*Zikar*), in reading and reciting Holy Qur'an nor in debating obstruse points of theology or theosophy. The Sufis felt what all one should ask for from God is love, the spark of love that enables one to recognize God within oneself.[76] They felt that one discovers in ones consciousness the action of Divine consciousness, whereby the Divine discovers through ones discovery of God, they find themselves once again. The Sufi asks, "Why seek for the known when you can know the knower?" This idea deeply appealed to Akbar and stood alongside his growing recognition of God in all beings.

At this time, Akbar felt it was necessary to instruct the members of the *Din-i-Illahi* (the Religion of One Light in the ten foundational virtues that he expected all to follow as members. They are:

1. Liberality and beneficence toward human beings and creatures
2. Forbearance from bad actions and repulsion of anger with mildness.
3. Abstinence from worldly desires.
4. Freedom from the bonds of worldly existence, [freedom from] violence as well as freedom from accumulating precious goods from the future real and perpetual world.
5. Piety, wisdom and devotion in the frequent meditations on the consequences of actions.
6. Strength of dexterous prudence in the desire of sublime actions. Meaning doing good works
7. Soft voice, gentle words, pleasing speech for everyone as well as creatures
8. Good society with brothers, so that their will [perspective] may have precedence to our own.

---

[76] Alam Khan, 1999.Pgs. 51-56

9. A perfect alienation [Meaning equanimity] from creatures and perfect attachment to the Supreme Being.
10. Purification of the soul by yearning after God, the "All-just," and union with the merciful Lord in such a manner that as long as the soul dwells in the body, it may think itself one with Him, until the hour of separation from the body arrives. The best men are those who content themselves with the least food and who sequestrate themselves from the perishable world, and abstain from the enjoyment of eating, drinking, dress and marriage.[77]

The ten virtues were proposed and members of *the Din-i-Illahi* who were more like kindred spirits were expected to follow them along with Akbar. The virtues were understood as a counter-balance against any fanaticism that might arise. The gathering was in the nature of a society of seekers of Truth rather than of a religion.[78] All members of the "new religion" or "The Religions of One Light" *(Din-i-Illahi),* being disciples of his Majesty Akbar, were expected to pay particular attention to every virtue, while keeping their own religion. The virtues then became a shared creed, and inculcated monotheism with a tinge of pantheism.[79]

The practical deification of the emperor as the vice-regents of God added power to the question of whether he was the awaited *Mahdi*. With ideas concerning the millennium and the expected appearance of the *Mahdi* being then discussed in the gathering, and with the year 1,000 of the Hijra approaching in the lunar calendar, arrangements were made for the compilation of a history of the past thousand years. Special measures were followed, beards were shaved, garlic, onions and beef were prohibited. All rules of Islamic protocol such as prostrations at prayer *(sijdah),* the old prohibition of wearing silk dresses to public prayer, required pilgrimage *(Hajj)* as well as the mandatory study of Arabic letters were discouraged. The gist of these new regulations was to integrate Hindu, Jain and Parsee practices without persecuting either those Muslim members who

---

[77] Krishnamurti, 1961. P. 109,110.
[78] Ibid. P.111
[79] Smith, 1958, 1962,1966. P.158.

strictly followed Islamic ritual practice,[80] or those on the other side, who did not follow ritual prayer.

Akbar needed the support of the Sufis in the gathering because he wanted to awaken the listeners from their doctrinal slumber and habit of disrespectful attitudes toward each other. Some members of the Empire resisted his innovations and would build sympathetic circles representing a rebellious force. Akbar maintained harmony by banishing his most virulent opponents to Sind and Kandahar, but he did not hold animosity against them or enslave them in any way. He kept returning to the ultimate reason why he brought everyone together,

> " My sole object Oh, wise Mullas, [of all paths] is to ascertain the Truth, to find out and disclose the principle of genuine religion and to trace it to "origin." Take care, therefore, that through the influence of your human passions you are not induced to conceal the Truth and say nothing contrary to the Almighty decrees. If you do, you are responsible before God for the consequence of your impiety."[81]

In the sessions of religious discourse in the *Ibadatkhana,* Akbar entered his destined element/station. He remained focused on the equality of all religions even in the face of strong opposition. He tried his best to hear everyone's perspective and attempted to keep a balance between speakers. No one person was allowed to dominate verbally and he hoped that unity of perspective might be realized. Having learned a great deal from Hinduism, Akbar followed a teaching in the Upanishads. The more one concentrates on unity, even though the apparent field of compass in the concentration narrows, the greater becomes the outlook.[82]

As the dialogues began, Akbar had to hold singularly the vision of unity as he attempted to guide the many to the One ideal. While a Muslim he boldly rejected Islamic law as the only primary doctrine, including both the Qur'anic revelations and the traditional sayings

---

[80] Ibid. P. 159
[81] Ibid. P.168
[82] Sufi Pir Hidayat Inayat Khan, head of the Sufi Movement International of the USA.

of Muhammad (*Hadith*). He found the Muslim followers rejecting of other religious doctrines, breaking the respectful spirit of fairness and the Qur'anic ethical command of justice (*ihsan*). The Sunni Mullas quarreled among themselves so violently they even drew 'swords of the tongue' among themselves. This grievous act gave Akbar further motivation to bring in more representatives of the many other religious groups in the community. It was at this point that he refreshed his interest in Christianity born during his time in Bengal.

CHAPTER 12

The Jesuit Christians

The missionary Father Monserrate was invited from Goa and attended the debates and dialogues hosted by Akbar. He was of a refined nature and educated in the idea that the Sacred Christian Gospel, having been foretold in the Holy Jewish Torah, must be superior to the Holy Qur'an, as there was no evidence in other scriptures that Islam would rise up through the Prophet Muhammad (*SAAwS*). The Jesuits also brought arguments that Mohammed had acknowledged the divine origin of the Christian Gospel, but he was inconsistent about his acknowledgment of the divinity of Christ.[83] These were blistering issues that brought great intensity to the debates.

Compounding the doctrinal differences between Christians and Muslims, there arose a political issue that Akbar was forced to address at this time. He was aware that the orthodox Sunni *'ulama* held many important civil and judicial assignments throughout the Mogul dominions. These appointed *'ulama,* such as Badaoni were solidly against Akbar's liberal rule as Emperor and felt that Mulla Mubarak led Akbar away from the traditional codes of Islam. Badaoni did not appreciate the open meetings with their spirit of controversy and Akbar's method of bringing in contrary perspectives that often revealed frozen concepts held by the religious pundits. Tension mounted as Akbar maintained full religious powers as *Iman-i-Adil* and he refused to be undermined or discouraged

As Christian representation was growing stronger with the arrival of Ridolfo Aquaviva and Francisco Enriquez joining Father Antonio Monserrate, a strange restraint was building in the voice of the *'ulama*. They observed how Akbar gave resident housing to the Fathers built them a Chapel for their worship service and allowed them to carry out sacred duties without fear. He even had copies of the Christian Bible distributed to the *'ulama* making it appear that his conversion to Christianity was imminent. The Jesuits also mistook Akbar's courtesy as submission. But when a second Christian missionary team came to Fatephur Sikri headed by Edward Leioton and Jerome Xavier, they were

---

[83] Krishnamurti, 1961 Pgs. 42-58.

disappointed to find Akbar's interest had turned to other faiths such as those of the Zoroastrians and the Jains.

It was a most propitious occasion when the Zoroastrian priest, Dastur Meharji Rana from Gujarat offered to teach Akbar the ceremonial practice of fire worship. Thereafter Akbar began to occupy his devotions each day with bowing to the Sun and keeping the fire burning in the royal courtyard for twenty-four hours a day. He called it "the perpetual flame" and Abul Fazl was entrusted with keeping it ablaze.[84] Akbar's worship of the sun should not be confused with idol worship. He saw nothing improper with the veneration of an exalted element as Abul Fazl quotes Akbar saying,

> "Every flame is derived from that fountain of light (the sun), and bears the impression of its holy essence. If light and fire did not exist, we should be destitute of food and medicines; the power of sight would be of no avail to the eyes. The fire of the sun is the torch of God's sovereignty." [85]

Akbar was happy to find out that reverence was shown to the sun not only in Zoroastrian practices but also in Hinduism, and by the Prophet Mohammed (*SAAwS*) himself.

During one of the debates, Akbar witnessed how unbalanced the *'ulama* were becoming, showing fanatic tendencies in their arguments and challenging the Jesuits to a drastic test of which religion was best. A member of the *'ulama* said, "Well, if you have faith let us decide the issue by a walk through a blaze of fire. You will carry the Bible in your hand, and I shall trust my fate to the Qur'an. Whosoever comes out unscathed will be the winner. Allah is my witness. I am prepared to die for my faith in the Prophet."[86]

Such debate seemed only to evoke emotional fixations that impeded Akbar's objectives. Antiquated concepts appeared to Akbar as having often locked the minds and hearts of the participants. He could find few solutions for maintaining fairness and courtesy to all

---

[84] Lal, 1980, P. 223
[85] Fazl, (Vol I), P. 48
[86] Ibid. P. 222

involved without utilizing his Imperial powers. Some of the Christian fathers thought that Akbar wanted everyone to go through a trial by fire in hopes that the ordeal would bring an opening. "After all Akbar was a rationalist," they said, "and he thinks that everything can be grasped by reasoning."[87]

This thought of the Christian fathers was far from the truth as Akbar had a keen understanding that had been mystically attuned by the Sufi masters. He knew that the Christian fathers saw Mohammed as a false prophet because they believed he would not appear at the end of the world as the advocate of humankind. The eschatological belief that it was Christ's mission to appear on the last Day of Judgment caused the Jesuit fathers to see no benefit in Qur'an. When this information got out to the people of the Empire, they would throw excrement at the Jesuit fathers as they walked through the streets to protest that they had spoken with disrespect about the life and teachings of the Prophet whom they loved. For this reason, the Jesuit fathers had to be subdued when in debates by Abul Fazl who advised they use caution and respect when speaking of any other faith thereafter.

Akbar's love for the Prophet remained an intimate connection to the Divine and Muhammad was his example of the perfect man. He saw the Prophet in his heart as one who submitted to becoming an instrument of God's will on earth. Unlike the *'ulama* who exteriorized the manner of the Prophet by holding to the general requirements of the faith *(fiqih)*, Akbar internalized the practice of the Prophet and saw himself rather as a vice-regents *(Mujtahid)*, who was empowered to depart from rules without committing a transgression. He understood kingship as being a divine fiat for serving the truth and that his subjects expected no less as rules that were common among the people *(Shariat)* were not immutable.

Determined to find a way to solve the problem of the *'ulama's* extremism, Akbar placed his children under the tutorship of the Jesuits and particularly into the care of Father Monserrate. This was a huge leap of faith because he always remained troubled by the

---

[87] Krishnamurti, 1961. P. 51

concept of "Trinity" and the main tenet of Christianity that God had only one son whom he considered the only embodiment of Himself. However, Akbar felt the Jesuit fathers were exceedingly erudite and well informed about the customs and religious scripture of other religious traditions, unlike the *'ulama* who showed no interest to learn of other religions than their own. Yet, always fair-minded and open to inclusion and synthesis of ideas, he assigned Faizee, who had been awarded the title of poet-laureate (*Maliku 'shi-shu'ara*), to continue tutoring the princes at the same time they were being educated by the Jesuits. Faizee was a master teacher of Arabic and Persian, and a respected Islamic scholar[88] and translator of many religious scriptures. Akbar saw the depth of synthesis that his sons could bring forward into their reign, hoping they would continue his spiritual innovations after his death.

Akbar not only kept the devotional practices of Zoroastrian worship of the sun regular in his daily observance, he was also faithful to all Persian holidays. He installed the Persian celebrations *Nawruz-i-Jalali* (New Years) and the feast days of *Farwardin, Urdibihisht, Khurdad, Amurdad, Shahriwar, Mihr, Aban, Azar, Bahman, Isfandarmuz* and also *Khushroz*, (the day of fancy bazaars). These festivities gained considerable enthusiasm in his court as did the Hindu religious ceremonies such as *Dussehra* (Triumph of good over evil) *Diwali* (Celebration of Light in honor of Rama and his consort) and *Holi* (Celebration of Spring and the New Year).

Akbar had begun formulating new ideas for his people when he was still very young bringing major concept changes to benefit members of the community by eradicating those customs that held ancient bias. Before Akbar was twenty years old, he had lifted the pilgrim tax (*Jizya*), and now in his later years, he also revoked the Hindu tax on pilgrims at Muttra and other holy places. After his experiences at Chitor he also wanted to eradicate the practice of *sati* (when a wife of a deceased husband throws herself on his funeral pyre). Historians say, that he once rushed fifty miles to save Raja Jamal's wife, who was the daughter of Rana Uday Singh's family and whose reputation of being a

---

[88] Alam Khan, 1999, P.198.

great beauty was legendary throughout Hindustan. After her husband died, Akbar stopped her from immolation by inviting her to join his harem.

A myth circulated throughout the Empire among the Hindu people that described the popular thinking about Akbar. Generous actions such as Akbar's invitation to the Rana's daughter became famously talked about, and many believed he was the reincarnation of some Hindu saint or god. A song was written about Akbar with uplifting imagery that pleased him, and spread among the people. The song follows:

> "The atrocities of Muslim rulers against their Hindu subjects galled him. He was pious and learned. People respected him for his courage and wisdom. His name was Mukand Brahamchai. He yearned for liberation from the Muslim yoke. His trust in God being firm, he staged a ritual (*yagya*) to invoke Him and ask that he be born a Kshatriya warrior in the next life. His wish was granted, but only partially. A mistake in the ceremonial of the *yagya* led to his being born a Muslim King. He is Akbar Padshah, the kind-hearted monarch who looks after Hindus and Muslims with equal love. He is a rishi, a holy man who looks upon his subjects with the eye of impartiality. Akbar is great. Let us praise him with our heart and soul."[89]

Akbar was devoted to his own practices and respectful to all creeds. He matured in his years and tested himself with the different religious austerities to see how they refined his knowledge of devotional matters (*ibadat*), and how they clarified his understanding of civil transactions (*muamalat*). For example, he banned the hunting of wild animals as sport, and he released all contained animals particularly birds from their cages. He believed that no creature should be inhibited by confinement, which was against its natural state. He was against the slaughter of animals for ritual sacrifice and wrote a law penalizing those who continued to carry out such rites. He became a vegetarian and attempted to follow Jain precepts yet he respected those who did not follow his dietary protocol and declared certain days of the week when meat could be consumed.

---

[89] Lal, 1980, P.226

The prohibitions concerning animals were recorded and mandated for the extended community with threatened punishments if disobeyed. The protection of animals was one issue he threw his regal weight behind as his love for animals always liberated his spirit and he respected the honesty of their relationship with humankind. They were, after all, his teachers in his youth.

Harmlessness (*Ahimsa*) appealed to Akbar as refraining from killing, hurting and injuring not only saved animals but would save himself and others from the sin of an evil act against so grand a creation of the Divine as the human being. As the great warrior King remembered how haunted he was by his experiences at Chitor and the image of the harem women of Baz Bahadur who committed suicide, he considered abstaining from killing as a kindness to oneself. Life was now more precious to him. He was still haunted by his past, and slowly exposing those in his Empire to a greater idea of protection of humankind became his ultimate aim. Abul Fazl confirms this in his chronicles:

> "The inspiration came to his holy heart that he would stretch out his hand slowly and by degrees so that things might not be made difficult for followers of the truth, and that constant apprehensions might not make the general public crazy."[90]

Akbar felt the moral weight of his killing sprees and spoke to his people as one who knew from the depth of his psyche how the soul is weighed down by actions that harm others. Abul Fazl's documents recorded how his Emperor was influenced by the great Jain sage, Hariji Sur (Hiravijaya Suri). Abul Fazl met with him many times and their discussion of theological matters proved that he was worthy to meet with the Emperor. Suri believed that true religion should be lived by compassion (*daya*) and that there is but one God although called by different names. Suri also expatiated on the nature of God and the true Guru. He asked the Emperor to release all caged birds and prisoners and stop the sacrificial slaughter of animals, particularly on the eight sacred Jain holidays

---

[90] Fazl, (Vol. III) P. 332

(*Paryushana*).⁹¹ As Akbar had already taken some of these actions, he felt confirmed in his commitment to continue along these altruistic lines.

Akbar so admired Heravijaya Suri that he was given the title of World Preceptor (*Jagadguru*) because he not only transmitted the knowledge of Jainism to the emperor but he also received various concessions to his religion in the form of residual laws (*farmans*) to promote non-killing.

In the year 1590, Akbar abolished taxes upon the Jains. The influence of Suri and other Jain teachers reached such proportions as to arouse the jealousy of the chief Brahmans in the court. But the great Hindu teacher and friend Brahmachandra (Birbal), who had composed one thousand names for the Sun which Akbar read every morning, understood Akbar's desire to learn from the Jains. Suri remained in Akbar's favor as a trusted advisor for forty-five years because of the deep compassion he exuded to all people he met.

Preceeding the abolishment of taxes to the Jain community, in the period around 1582, Akbar gave honors to the inner group of devoted representatives that surrounded him and who understood the synthesis of his religious experiment toward "divine oneness" (*Tawheed-i-llahi*). They were the primary advocates of his vision and search for the Light of One God in many forms in the "new religion" or "divine faith" (*Din-i-Illahi*). The members were:

    Abul Fazl
    Abul Faiz Faizee
    Sheikh Mubarak (father of Abul Fazl, and Faizee)
    Ja'far Beg Acef Khan
    Qasim-i-Kaki (a poet)
    Abdul Samad (poet and painter)
    Aziz Khan Kaka
    Mulla Shah Muhammed (historian)
    Sufi Ahmed Qadr Jahan (lawyer)

---

⁹¹ Krishnamurti, 1961. P. 75

- Akbar's two sons Salim and Murad
- Mir Sharif of A'mul
- Sultan Khwajah
- Mirza Jani Taqi of Shustar (poet)
- Shaikhzadah Gosilah of Benares
- Raja Brahmachandra Birbal

It is interesting to note that all members who he esteemed were Muslims except for Raja Brahmachandra Birbal, a Hindu. The Muslim representatives could not have participated unless Akbar showed enormous respect and reverence to the essential precepts of Islam. All the members of the *Din-i-Illahi* recognized in Akbar a highly qualified Muslim advocate of spiritual law and the Sufis saw Akbar as a true brother.

But his ultimate mission was always a bit out of reach and always before him. The quandary of finding the right formula for bringing through the principles of "unity in diversity" was his aim for the gathering. He pushed on through open discourse and debate and refused to intercept the difficult encounters that would arise between the challenging opponents. He rather trusted in the evolution of the dialogue process, hoping that if a problem surfaced a solution would reveal itself. To find out if his method was working, he made further inquiries into the general population. He was interested to see if the people benefited from these weekly discussions, which the leaders brought back into their mosques, churches, synagogues and temples. He found to his disappointment that the community was still locked in habituated religious rituals and supported the orthodox and conservative perspectives of their religious leaders rather than those represented through the *Din-i-Illahi*.

Realizing the obstacles for change that the general population was facing he lowered his expectations. He realized it would take time for the conditioned belief systems, which were embedded over many generations within the many cultures populating his Empire to evolve. He could see from the contentious dialogues with the most learned men of his period that he had to wait and refine his efforts.

So he turned his attention to those members he could handle immediately, the religious leaders. Muslim pundits were linked to powerful positions in the hierarchy of the Empire, and they perceived his openness to other religious leaders as a devious action to oust them from power. . The externals of ritual practices of Islamic doctrine such as prayer, style of dress, and submission to the five pillars of Islamic ethics without investigation, were emphasized repeatedly in community services. Akbar felt that these ritual observances were rooted in fear, and that the *'ulama* were using fear to control their people. Within the Muslim community (*ummah*), peace and harmony were not a priority, and hostile sects continued to war against each other. The Sunnis, the Shias, and the Mahdevis entered brutal conflicts that caused Akbar persistent problems. The conflicts validated his notion that the Islamic community was not essentially following the Shari'ah which guided the individual in the following principles:

1) The declaration of faith (Ilm), *La El La Ha El Allah Hu, Mohammad-a-Rassoul Lillah*. (There is no reality only/except God and Mohammed is God's messenger.)
2) Charity (Zakat), giving 2% of what one earns to the greater community.
3) Prayers (Salat), maintaining the five rounds of prayers each day which coordinate with the movement of the sun.
4) Fasting (Ramadan), a time of deep inner examination and renunciation of food during the sunlight hours of the day.
5) Pilgrimage (Hajj), the time of greatest devotion and travel to Mecca in gratitude for the Holy Ones who gave us the true message.

Akbar's close minister Abdun Nabi Severe, who replaced Bairam Khan in taking the Imperial authority of Khan-i-Khanan, caused further injustice because of his extreme hatred for the Shia population. He shunned the Mahdavis as heretics and did everything in his power to prevent Akbar's ideas for the *Din-i-Illahi* to move forward.

The self-righteousness of the disputing Muslim pundits convinced Akbar once again of the *'ulama's* unfitness to be representatives of the true values of Islam. Though deeply depressed by their indiscretions, Akbar never lost his temper and sought to pacify their rising passions by asking them to use their intellect rather than their emotions when sharing their perspectives with others. It appeared to them that he was trying to dissuade Islamic representation and was turning against the religion of his ancestry. But Akbar's love for Islam was a guarded treasure that continually informed his direction as he submitted to the inner practice of *"Ihsan"*[92] which he felt was the essential state of sincerity and conviction in ones practice to realize being in the Divine Presence.

---

[92] *Ihsan* relates to faith, indicating the sincerity of ones conviction. *Iman* and *Islam* are often used interchangeably but *Iman* means a belief in Allah, the angels and messengers (which includes the Books and the Messages) *(Liqa-Allah)*, while *Islam* means the worshipping *(ibadah)* of Allah and submission to God's will, maintaining prayers, fasting in the month of Ramadan, Zakat and Hajj. The person who accepts these principles is a Muslim and a member of the Muslim *ummah*.

CHAPTER 13

Spiritual Authority and the Mahzer

The critical issue that arose historically, causing Akbar great trouble with the *'ulama*, was concerning a document that went out recognizing Akbar's spiritual authority, (*Mahzer*),[93] which the orthodox Sunni community propagated wrongly. They attacked Akbar's motivation in the *Din-i-Illahi* to oust Islam as a primary religion, indicating, naturally, that they would follow Islam's demise and be removed from power. This was an incorrect assumption on their part. He was accused of combining the role of spiritual and temporal leader, an act never before done by a Mogul emperor. After the *Mahzer* was announced, Akbar did everything he could to counter any maligning opinion. As many time as the issue arose concerning his spiritual authority, the more he had to use the rights given to him in the *Mahzer*.

A secondary issue along attached to the subject of the *Mahzer* caused complications for Akbar as a general misconception continued to spread, which historians have held for decades as true. The secondary issue began over Akbar's seal (*Shast*). This was a metal disk, bearing on one side Akbar's name and the other the Islamic *Kalma* (Literally meaning the "Word"), God is Great (*Allah-Hu-Akbar*). The highest members of the *Din-i-Ilahi* (Religion of the One Light), were to keep this disk inside their turbans as a reminder and sign of authority if they needed to show it for any reason.

In view of the dual setting in the seal, of Akbar's names and God's name side by side, the *'ulama* assumed Akbar was taking the role of the Prophet Muhammad (*SAAwS*) who was the only one who had Divine proximity. Akbar's *Shast* represented a symbol that ran counter to the injunction of Islam. Although Akbar regarded his *Shast* as a blessing given to him by the *Kalma* next to his name, unfortunately this belief that he was about to

---

[93] Srivastava, 1998, P.170. The Mahzer was a proclamation prepared in 1579 by Sheikh Mubarak recognizing Akbar in his capacity as not only Supreme Monarch but as Amir-ul-Momin and Iman-I-Adil. The Mahzer confirmed that Akbar was given religious right to govern not only civil matters but religious matters as well. He could exercise these rights only when the Muslim 'ulama failed to arrive at agreements which was the majority of the time.

subvert Islam by assuming the Prophet's position, pervaded his reign.[94] Akbar assumed he was the supreme arbiter of disputes (*Sultan-i-Adil*), but he never assumed he was in the same league as the Holy Prophet Muhammad (*SAAwS*). His aim had always been to respect Islam and work as an interpreter (*Mahdi*) with its tenants.

Considering this controversy with many Muslim opponents, and an unusual a turn in his unfolding history opened. The *'ulama* appointed Akbar as the *Iman-ul-Iman* giving him privileges to interpret spiritual law as well as jurisprudence. The following document is of great significance as a historic defense of Akbar's true intentions.

> "Now we, the principle *'ulama* who are not only well-versed in the several departments of the Law and in the principles of jurisprudence, and well acquainted with the edicts which rest on reason or testimony, but are also known for our piety and honest intentions, have duly considered the deep meaning, first, of the verse of the Qur'an.
>
> 'Obey God, and obey the Prophet, and those who have authority among you'; and secondly, of the genuine tradition. 'Surely the man who is dearest to God on the day of judgement is the *Imam-i-Adil*; whosoever obeys the Amir, obeys Thee; and whosoever rebels against him, rebels against thee';
>
> And secondly, of several other proofs based on reasoning or testimony: and we have agreed that the rank of *Sultan-i-Adil* is higher in the eyes of God than the rank of a *Mujtahid*. Further, we declare that the King of Islam, Amir of the Faithful, Shadow of God in the world, Abul-Fath, Jalal-ud-Din Muhammad Akbar, Padshah Ghazi (whose kingdom God perpetuate!), is a most just, a most wise, and a most God-fearing king.
>
> Should, therefore, in future a religious question come up, regarding which the opinions of the *Mujahids* are at variance, and His Majesty, in his penetrating

---

[94] Lal, P. 229

understanding and clear wisdom be inclined to adopt, for the benefit of the nation and as a political expedient, any of the conflicting opinions which exist on that point, and should issue of decree to that effect. We do hereby agree that such a decree shall be binding on us and on the whole nation.

Further, we declare that should His Majesty think fit to issue a new order, we and the nation shall likewise be bound by it; provided always, that such order be not only in accordance with the some verse of the Qur'an, but also of real benefit to the nation; and further, that any opposition on the part of his subjects to such an order passed by His Majesty shall involve damnation in the world to come and loss of property and religious privileges in this.

This document has been written with honest intentions for the glory of God and the propagation of Islam, and is signed by us, the principle *'ulama* and lawyers, in the month of *Rajab* in the year nine hundred and eighty-seven."[95]

It was evident that not all the *'ulama* stood against Akbar's powers of persuasion. Some did see that he had a deep respect for the Prophet Mohammed (*SAAwS*) and that his heart and soul were rooted in the underlying rationale, effective cause, and purpose of Islam. There was an instance that proved his devotion, when Abu Turab returned from pilgrimage (*Hajj*) from Mecca, and brought a stone with the impression of the Prophet's foot on it as a gift to his King. Akbar went out several miles to receive the relic,[96] as he was overjoyed at the presentation of the Holy item. Another moment offering insight to his fidelity, was in how he respected the parents of the Prophet as well as his progeny far more deeply than others. This was shown during the year 1564 when one of his wives gave birth to twins. To show his devotion to the Prophets legacy, Akbar named the twins, Mirza Hasan and Mirza Husain.[97]

---

[95] Lal, P.230
[96] Badaoni, II p. 320 Tabaqat-I-Akbari, II, P. 558.
[97] Fazl, (Vol. II) 1977, P.236. Husan and Husain were the sons of the Prophet's daughter, Fatimah and his son in law Ali.

There is a legend regarding Akbar's obvious devotion to the Prophet that takes place sometime in 1573. A Transoxian preacher, Maulana 'Abdur Rahman, spoke in the course of his sermon in the Friday Mosque of Fatehpur Sikri, about the infidelity of the parents of the Prophet and their being consigned to hell. Akbar disagreed with it and told the congregation:

> "Methinks this statement is not true, for when there has been intercession for so many offenders by this means [the Prophet], how can the father and mother be excluded, and be consigned to everlasting infidelity?"[98]

The audience applauded Akbar for his views. The people realized his deep love for the Holy Prophet and understood how much the living legacy of Islam was apparent in his inherent manner of respectfulness (*adab*).

Yet the effort of constantly proving his fidelity to orthodox followers of Islam was a difficult task for a seeker such as Akbar who questioned everything. After studying the many religions and hearing the various perspectives from the different leaders, Akbar finally came to the realization that he had to seek the answers from within his own reality, freed of any doctrinal crutch. It was at this juncture that he once again turned to the Sufis and bowed to the deep knowledge and wisdom they found through their interior knowledge (*mar'ifa*) that informed their direct tasting of experiences (*dhwaq*). The Sufi's never proselytize or coerced others to build their membership. They rather formed their solidarity by following a path of complete denial of the self (*fana*) and by surrendering the ego (*nafs*) to God. The Sufis became the "Illahi", the ultimate Divine attribute of Akbar's new order. Their pragmatic existence (*baqa*) of priorities aimed at transforming the Mogul empire into a brotherhood of humanity from the inside out, rather than the other way around. In total accord with Akbar's reasoning and transformation of his heart, this was an end that was its own justification.

---

[98] Fazl, (Vol. III), 1977 P. 74

He was certain, upon having this realization, that he was essentially the one chosen Mogul emperor given the task to bring this message with the help of Dervishes. He was inspired by the inner luminosity of his own realizations, but the Sufis opened his heart to the panorama of uniqueness within unity and the responsibility that each individual has to uncover the divine privilege of inner knowledge (*kashf*) and transform their consciousness. He knew that the inner knowledge (*kashf*) was the only means through which true and trustworthy knowledge could be attained. The Sufis described it, as a light with which God floods into the heart of the believer. No longer did he want boundaries that limited his vast oceanic possibilities for love, wisdom and understanding. He wanted to recognize that all he knew was what he ever imagined knowing.

Again, as before, although Akbar planted the seed of interfaith tolerance, firm opposition pressed against his efforts. Historians have commented on his difficulties by saying that the *Tawhid-i-Illah* (the official name for the *Din-i-Ilahi*), had no metaphysical or even ethical foundation. No religious philosophy sustained it and no higher moral or spiritual values buttressed its unifying perspective. Those with negative commentary said his efforts were an agglomeration of certain rituals, whimsically visualized and pompously demonstrated. [99] As corollary historic records prove, this was far from the truth. The need for a broad humanitarian approach towards all people, regardless of their faith or creed is the ethical core and strength of a great community. This was the ideal that Akbar and the Sufis were proposing and they were doing it without formulating another doctrine. This was truly a visionary jump into the future for what in contemporary terms could be called, "Interfaith" understanding today. Akbar did not allow these naysayers to prevail. He was certain that doctrinal systems hiding as a spiritual path were contradictory to heart awakening. The illusory intellect alone could be used to destroy trust in human logic and the potential for harmony which was essential for attaining a true sense of peace with all (*sulk-i-kul*) needed a unifying context and practice.

Inspired by his visions of unity (*Tawhid*) and coupled with his inherent rebellion against boundaries, he identified with those who were struggling spiritually. He observed from

---

[99] Nizami, 1989. P.133

the Sufi Orders (*tariqats*) that training in self-discipline was necessary. Liberation from the ego and its fixations required practices. Akbar realized he needed to educate disciples in the manner (*adab*) of tolerance, as dialogue (*itjihad*) was not effective enough. Apparent in the Sufi communities, where non-compulsive acts of devotion and prayer were evident in their practices, the Sufis were always attuning themselves to spontaneously arrive at ecstatic states through contemplative observation (*muraqabah*). These Sufi methods inspired Akbar to create some outward rituals that he could teach the members of the *Din-i-Illahi* to use in daily life. He formulated simple ceremonial prescriptions such as:

> "In the morning, the midday, at sunset and at midnight, prayers were enjoined. The sun and fire were the objects of veneration, and everybody was expected to rise when the lamps were lit in the evening. No manifestation of God was as effulgent and sacred as the sun; hence the desirability of doing it obeisance in the morning. In 1583, an edict of complete tolerance was issued; all those who had been converted to Islam by force were allowed to re-embrace the religion of their birth. Marriages of near-relatives, such as cousins, were prohibited. Boys were not to marry before their sixteenth and girls before their fourteenth year. The Islamic injunction against the wearing of silken robes at the time of prayers was withdrawn. To the long list of the festivals of Hindustan were added the fourteen festivals of Persia; all citizens of the Empire were expected to attend these festivals. Friday prayers were obligatory on all Muslims. The old Persian names of the months were brought back into use. The study of Arabic was no longer compulsory. On the other hand the study of astronomy, philosophy, medicine, mathematics, poetry, history, and the fine arts was encouraged. High priests of all religions were required to attend the Persian *Nauroz* (New Year) feast. Leading linguists, including Badaouni, were commissioned to translate into Persian the holy books of all religions; copies were made available to scholars for consultation. Slaughter of animals was prohibited on Sundays and in the month of the Emperor's birth. In the winter, the Emperor wore clothes made of white (*suf*)

raw wool, and expected the like-minded courtiers and common citizens to do the same."[100]

Members of the *Din-i-Illahi* had to vow discipleship to the Emperor, follow the above principles, and serve the needs of educating others so that the *Din-i-Illahi* would grow. It is said that Akbar's disciples did not increase over one thousand and upon Akbar's death, his efforts evaporated as the community quickly fell back into prescribed fundamental practices found in Hinduism and Islam.

The unfortunate ending of Akbar's interfaith vision, coupled with the moral breakdown of Akbar's son Salim who was to become the Jahangir, many of his inspired ideas quickly evaporated from the Mogul court. Some of the great master teachers who gathered in his circle did appreciate the spiritual wisdom that Akbar brought through his efforts. But sadly, upon the change of power, and the elderly age of those who were dying off, the foundation of his original experiments for building a nation dedicated to interfaith tolerance did not hold past his lifetime.

The search for the elements of unity (*Tawhid*) in Indian cultural life had been emphasized by such Sufi masters mentioned earlier as: Khwaja Moineddin Chisthi of Ajmer, Sheikh Hamid-u-ddin Sufi of Nagour, Sheikh Nizamuddin Auliya of Delhi and Amir Khusrau and others. But none of these masters had contributed to the vision of interfaith expression as profoundly as Akbar. Against the background of religious fundamentalism, even they could not revive solace, nor inspiration from the interfaith and semi-metaphysical values Akbar had formulated. The Sufis rather maintained their unique practices and stayed focused on what they had found as the pathway for supplicating the false ego (*nafs*) to the real (*fana*). Except for the spiritual principle of unity (*Tawhid*) that all life was a reflection of the Divine, the Sufis recognized Akbar as a unique spiritual contributor. Akbar's attempt to reach for inter-religious solutions went far beyond the historic time frame that could accept them. He was a King who speaks to the future.

---

[100] Lal, 1980, P.233

All religions doctrines, according to Akbar, needed re-evaluation so that the laws that kept human ethics in check would not succumb to the impending calamity of being proven worthless. His greatest disappointment was indeed manifested. Without Akbar's charismatic personality to drive the initiative, of tolerance (*sulk-i-kul*) and the energy to pursue seeking the wisdom living in all doctrines, the longevity of his vision faltered. His hope to find in all faiths, "The religion of One Light" (*Din-I-Illahi*), the generation he brought this message to could not understand it. It was given into the hands of the future.

Although Akbar began his life as a warrior, he ended it as a mystic. He wanted all faiths to flower in fairness and peace. He had paid a high price born from his episodes of killing, which birthed his desire to change the Timurid legacy. These two aspects culminated in a powerful shift of consciousness. He envisioned all people of all cultures living in dignity and respect of each other's differences. But the difficulties never ceased and the arguments never subsided during his reign. Abul Fazl says of Akbar's religious experiments,

> "Whenever from lucky circumstances, the time arrives that a nation learns to understand how to worship truth, the people will naturally look to their king on account of the high position which he occupies and expect him to be their spiritual leader as well."[101]

It was true that many religious leaders had great difficulty absorbing Akbar's religious experiments because he was an Emperor and as a ruler he was expected to fulfill secular duties. The pundit's never realized he could fulfill secular and spiritual duties. The Islamic pundits felt they would have to step down from their leadership and leave their lofty hierarchical positions within their faith system if they accepted Akbar's spiritual authority. Their egotistic response to Akbar's policy of tolerance (*sulk-i-kul*) that proposed open-mindedness threatened to disempower their positions in the community and for this reason they stood against him. A willingness to absorb another person's

---

[101] Fazl. Ain-I-Akbari. (tr.Blochmann), 1871,1965, P.182

perspective at the possible cost of losing ones own point of view, was too mystical an idea to be comprehended by those caught in rigid doctrines.

Religion had historically spread through coercive techniques and not by methods of tolerance. One could understand the confusion in the members of the *Din-i-Illahi* and the lack of readiness for this profound insight. However, as much as Akbar was criticized for playing the dual role of Emperor and Prophet, the *'ulama* did not speak their descent of his efforts to his face. Akbar's power was great and his persuasion even greater. They did fear him and they held their tongue concerning their doubts.

Even though courtly behavior demanded respectful protocol, Akbar's faith in the *'ulama* was constantly shaken due to how they had previously behaved in many of the sessions in the *Ibadatkhana*. The emotional outbursts of disrespect caused Akbar to have revulsion for the traditional values of any religious doctrine. Even Badaoni, holding true to Muslim ethics, while not in favor of Akbar's vision, did not take well to those members of *Ibadatkhana* who were outspoken and becoming enemies to Akbar's throne. Historians claim there was good reason behind Badaoni's faithfulness. "It was based on Akbar's efforts to create an Indian State – a state conterminous with all the Indian people. This idea was not resisted nor resented by the Muslim population of his day. In fact Badaoni understood this fact as a logical culmination of the processes working since the establishment of the Turkish rule in India.[102]

Akbar knew, as did the Sufis, that religious dialogue would assist humanity in its emancipation. As a king to his people, offering a place for open exchange of ideas was a practical way for dispelling built-up resentment. He was certain that unrepressed speech coupled with the ancient forces living through the teachings of the wise prophets would forge through the vicissitudes of fixated thinking. Even through the separating forces found in cultural, economic and political influences, one could surely find cohesive influences living in the scriptural texts from the many religions. Surely, the desire in

---

[102] Nizami, 1989, P.243.

people to bond together in a religious belief built a greater consistency of unity in the history of humankind than the bond of one's cultural habits, or so Akbar thought.

CHAPTER 14

Final departure from Fatephur Sikri

Akbar's unifying realization born on the wings of Sufi practice and manifested in his ten years of work at Fatephur Sikri came to an end at last when he was called again to the battlefield. The Pashtun rebel forces had capture Kabulistan. Munim Khan, the ruthless Uzbegian rebel chief, had risen to power and captured Bahar, Balkh, Samarkand, and Farghana. He remained a constant source of trouble to Akbar throughout the course of his later years. He even attempted to ask for Akbar's daughter in marriage, which Akbar refused. Insulted and filled with retaliatory rage, Munim Khan struck back killing thousands of Akbar's Imperial army.

With this tumult rising in the north-east another emotional blow shot its deepest arrow into Akbar's heart. Raja Birbal, his closest and most beloved friend, was killed. For Akbar's type of personality, who held such high regard for his beloved friend, he was never the same after Birbal died. Suffering days of deep grief, his hours of strategizing his conquest of Kabulistan could not distract him from sorrowing for the loss of his friend.

To compound his grief, Todar Mal, Akbar's first Hindu Prime Minister (*Vakil*), and whom some historians considered Akbar's alter-ego, died suddenly. Shortly after losing his Vakil, two more loving companions, Amir Abul Fateh and Todar Mal, all passed over within the same range of time.

The void of these loving companions greatly distracted Akbar. He considered them his pillars for a spiritual bridge that he would build to bring the Hindus and the Muslims together. They were the supportive voices he needed to sustain his efforts against doubters and to breakdown the barriers between religions and races. Without their emotional support, he fell into a swoon in which he refused meat and wine for forty-one days.

During Akbar's time of grieving, his son Salim fathered two sons and three daughters and Murad fathered one son. The event of his grandchildren did not do much to remove him from his sorrow although he loved Murad's son, Rustum above all the others. Attempting to pull himself out of his grief, Akbar decided to take obligatory trips to visit the dead to see if he could find solace as he had found before when he visited the Dargah of Moineddin Chisthi. He spent time at the tomb of Babar in Kabul and visited his uncle's tomb, Hindal at the same time. He found for the first time, that the pilgrimage did not relieve his heart of the absence of his beloved friends and supporters.

In 1592 at the age of fifty, he married the daughter of Shams Kahn Kak from Kashmir. This marriage distracted him for only a short period as he began to feel that it was necessary to conquer the areas of Tibet and Turan. He decided against expanding northwards when his counsel advised him about the inclement weather in the Himalayan terrain. He also had a previous dream that the angel of death had appeared to him. His vision halted his plans to the north and instead he redirected his energy to the Deccan in the south.

The majority of the Deccan population was Shi'ite. They were the descendent immigrants from Persia who had come to India via the western ports between the 12th and 13th Century. Prince Murad was made Governor of Malwa and Akbar had clear instructions for Murad prioritizing the moral values that would successfully reflect his administrative and Imperial position. He hoped that Murad, Daniyal and Salim who were all showing signs of rebellion through their debauchery would hold his legacy. His message to the Prince indicates the high standards from which Akbar lived and ruled and which he expected his sons to follow.

> It is important that action is taken after careful thought. In eating, clothing, sleeping and walking, men should seek to increase wisdom, and not the fattening of the body, or pleasure. In governing, the idea should be to protect the feeble from the strong arm of oppression. Improvement of the country and the army should be advanced. Company should always be kept with the good. Do not

associate with praters, loquacious persons, drunkards, foul-mouthed persons, buffoons, bad-hearted men, base people, the envious, ignorant sellers of wisdom, handsome youths and young women.

Do not turn away from the bitter disposition of the truthful and be not angry with them, nor be vexed on account of the superior enlightenment of the well intentioned. Consider abundance of well-wishing as an ornament of dominion, not as a reason for neglect. Judge nobility of cast and high birth from the personality, and not goodness from grandfathers, or greatness from the seed.

Study the daily doings and manners of your companions. Be intent in prayer. Do not let reprisals pass beyond bounds, and do not attend to such matters when angry or hungry. Be not offended by diversity of religion. Struggle hard to sit in the shade of peace with all. Do not stain your soul with revenge. Do not take the path of deceit when inflicting retribution. Keep secrets to yourself, and except to one or two right-thinking and profound persons do not reveal your thoughts. Do not refer deliberation to an unsuitable assemblage. First, inquire separately and then in full meeting. Do not indicate your (private) advisor.

Do not distress the relation, the intimate and the neighbor by angry glances. If a thing can be remedied by kindness, do not have recourse to terror. Do not seek the destruction of the fallen, nor follow up the flying. Do not open the lips to utter oaths. Receive warning from others, not from oneself. Whoever gathers wisdom from the teaching of the world learns without the learner's pain.

Forget not any one who does you service, and strive to recompense it. Postpone not to the morrow the work of today. Reckon a good name as eternal life. Keep aloof from jesting, and toying, especially with one who is higher (or older) than you.

Regard the shining sword and the pen as the two arms of power. Commit the first to the brave and frank-hearted, and the second to the contented and right acting. Soldiers get a great name by four things: first, loyalty to their master; second, love to their comrades; third, obedience; forth, experience. The general is famed who always looks after the pay, the arms and the cattle of his followers, and who is always prepared. And he wins their hearts by gifts of honors, and looks after the survivors of deceased soldiers."[103]

The moral requirements that Akbar gave to Murad proved too difficult. He was already addicted to opium and degenerated to the most degraded form of debauchery. Akbar tried to rally Murad by sending him an angry letter concerning his disobedience, but to no avail.

Even the death of Murad's son Rustum could not waken him from his drunken slumber and Akbar called in Salim and Daniyal to lead an expedition to Turan demanding that Murad accompany them. Akbar knew the trip would be hazardous. It was one thing to crush a rebellion of over zealous chiefs but another to overcome the threat of three rebellious sons. Akbar's intention was to bring them into submission. He believed that if he waged a successful victory in the south this would foster the allegiance of his sons Murad and Daniyal and then Salim would follow suit.

Daniyal came to Akbar first offering his apologies and asking forgiveness. He swore to abstain from all liquor and to observe the high code of conduct, which Akbar had articulated in his letter to Murad. But Murad and Salim remained obstinate. Salim did not want to get embroiled in a conquest because he had set his sights on taking over the throne at Akbar's death. He stayed at the frontiers of Rajasthan guarding its territory with the help of Raja Man Singh making the city of Ajmer another Mogul stronghold.

---

[103] Lal, 1980, Pgs.273, 274.

Despairing over Murad's refusal of obedience, Akbar sent in his close advisor, Abul Fazl to guide Murad to his senses. But before Abul Fazl reached him, Murad's heavy drug use led him into an irreversible epileptic seizure that killed him.

Murad's death did not surprise Akbar. He received the information with a stoic attitude knowing well those ten years of Murad's twenty-nine years were tempestuous. Akbar rather turned his attentions to Daniyal in the hope that he would bring the conquest in the south to fruition. Daniyal was entrusted with the conquered territories of Gujarat and Malwa becoming the ruling Viceroy of the Deccan with Abul Fazl as his supreme advisor.

Akbar left for Agra in September 16th, 1599. His grandson's Khusrau, Parvaz and Khurram (born 1591) who was to become the Shahjehan, were the son's of Prince Salim and Rani Balmati, daughter of the Rajput chieftain Mota Raja. His grandson's were his security plan to preserve the Timurid legacy in case his own son's faltered in their abilities to rule. Although Akbar was aware of his son's weaknesses, he felt they would out grow their addictions as he did. He felt that sovereign responsibilities would mature and the extravagance of decadent behavior would diminish. He did not know that he would lose two son's to drug abuse and that Salim would attempt to betray him and poison him.

Recognizing that the close of his reign was nearing, Akbar knew that this attempt to conquer the territories in the Deccan would be his last conquest. He regretted not succeeding in Bijapur, Galcona and Bidar, but news of Salim's outrageous proclamation that he was now Shahinshah and reigning Emperor at Allahabad necessitated Akbar's immediate departure from the southern territories.

As Akbar arrived in Agra, it was a somber affair and this is the historic point in which Abul Fazl's coverage in the <u>Akbar Nama</u>[104] stops. Akbar's beloved historian was on route to see Salim who detested Abul Fazl's influence and tolerant religious perspective, hired

---

[104] The Akbar Nama is the comprehensive courtly chronicle of Akbar's reign.

a paid assassin to kill him. Although news of a possible assassination plot had reach Abul Fazl before his departure, he refused taking a large private escort for his journey. On the morning of August 12th 1602, he and his escort met their death. Abul Fazl's head was severed and brought to Salim at Allahabad to prove the assassination attempt was completed.

It is said after the death of Abul Fazl, Inayatuallah Khan finished the historic document detailing the last four years of Akbar's life. Faizee had already passed on in 1597, two years after their father; Sheikh Mubarak had passed at the age of one hundred years old. These three men were the core philosophers who conceived and supported the great reformist work that Akbar established as a movement of tolerance (*Din-i-Illahi*) formatting the future code of peaceful coexistence (*Sulk-i-kul*). Without the support and presence of these men, the *Din-i-Illahi* began dying. Akbar reflected on whether he could maintain it alone and who would be the most worthy proponent for carrying the wise ideals of tolerance forward into the future.

It is confirmed historically that Abul Fazl and Faizee were the two great influences in Akbar's reign. They brought him the true appreciation of his duties as a King. As Sufis themselves, they honored the ideals of unity, which their Sufi lineages propounded. Some Muslim historians such as the powerful Badoani claimed that both the brother's were the influence that turned Akbar away from orthodox Islam. It is clear in the collective historical works written by the many scholars of Akbar's reign, that these two brother's not only brought the deep interfaith respect and tolerance which directed Akbar's effort for greater dialogue but they helped in uniting the vast groups of mixed races and creeds living in Hindustan. Their policy of toleration and respect were at the core of Sufi teachings that uplifted equality and hope for unity in a period of history that was embroiled in doctrinal battles.

Knowing that Faizee and Sheikh Mubarak were no longer his pillars of strength and guidance, and upon hearing of the death of his most beloved and intimate friend, Abul Fazl, Akbar fell into a swoon and lost consciousness. He would beat his breast often and would cry openly heaving sighs of pain. He never entirely forgave Salim for this act of viciousness against his trusted companion. During this grief stricken period, Akbar received news that Daniyal had returned to his drinking and that his health was deteriorating quickly. Daniyal fell into bed for forty days, remaining in a hopeless stupor never to revive.

Losing his sons under such circumstances, Akbar decided to make his court at Kashmir. He chose the palace of Yusuf Shah for his stay in Srinagár and wandered in the valley distracted for almost thirty-nine days. His reflections covered the many years of his reign. As he merged into the beauty of nature, he regained the pantheistic interconnectedness that he wished to promote as peace with all, (*Sulk-i-Kul*). He knew he had fulfilled the destiny given to him during his reign as predicted by his astrologers at his birth. He was so grateful for the companionship of those wise companions, the Sufis, who accompanied him throughout his reign. The ideals that he put forth in his *Din-I-Illahi* were the reflections of the great Sufi masters. He felt he did them honor as he held aloft their ideals and where the gifts to his people from a blessed King. His days at Fatephur Sikri were the most important and celebrated contributions of his life. Not only did he bring beauty through architectural structures, he designed a place where all cultures could live in harmony with nature. All these thoughts of accomplishment and gratitude filled his aching heart but he was grieved and troubled by the death of his two sons and the naked ambition of Salim.

Akbar's days in retrospection and tranquility were short lived. Salim was intensifying his estrangement. For almost a whole year due to the influence of an astrologer, Bairagi Ram Das, Akbar began to understand the nuances that plagued the relationship between father and son. He reflected on those faithful companions who were near and dear to him who showed far more fidelity then his own blood-line. He looked back at the betrayal of Maham Anaga and others in his family who would rather have preferred and inadequate son rule over that of himself. Or like Bairam Khan, once being a co-creator with his King, betrayed him by egotistically denying him support for his visionary ideals promoting religious tolerance.

Surrounded by family difficulties and deceit from his closest advocates, his son provided the deepest cut carrying forth a prediction by the Rajputs that Jodha Bai would have a hand in Akbar's downfall. This was an old score that needed to be settled and still haunted by his atrocities at Chitor, a karmic return was to reveal itself. It is written that supposedly Salim had made several earlier attempts to poison Akbar conspiring to get Hakim Ali, Akbar's doctor, to carry out the dreadful task. There is evidence that it could have been pollution through the effects of water and food that had earlier caused Akbar severe stomach disorders.[105] Salim was obviously impatient and he did not want to wait a longer period of time to take the throne, nevertheless, all attempts failed. Although the bulk of the Imperial army had been siding with Salim, Akbar was still considered the father of his people.

As fidelity in the community rose up in favor of Akbar, as a father he was confused about moving against his son, his cherished "Sheikh Baba," who he prayed for and who received the beloved Sheikh Salim's blessing (*baraka*) at his awaited birth. Coupled with this confusion, Akbar also knew that Salim was happy at Daniyal's death as competition for the throne was taken away from his certain ascendancy. Observing Salim for years, Akbar knew that his eldest son had developed into a coward and would not be able to withstand a concerted assault if Akbar chose to wage one. If Salim's rebellion continued he would have to consider placing Khusrau, Salim's oldest son in place to supersede the natural succession of Salim.

When Akbar returned to Agra in June of 1601, the capital was in a state of disarray. Salim's lustful pursuits had embroiled disharmonies, splitting the household into unforgiving hostilities against the throne. Akbar finally regained his emotional composure. He sent a firm letter to Salim demanding his obedience to his message. He desired only that Salim would be influenced by his command to rule as a wise king. Akbar's warning had no doorway for escape. In the letter, Salim was instructed to submit to Imperial command. If he did not comply with Akbar's wishes, the Imperial Forces

---

[105] Burke, 1989, fn. 41, (AN III, 1259-61)

would be used against him to bring him down. Akbar felt certain that if Salim did not clean himself up from his degraded behavior and defend the values of the house of Babar at this juncture, courtly born rebellion would destroy the entire legacy of the Timurid line.

The threat worked and Salim fled Agra for Allahabad. Frightened that this maneuver by his father would threaten his ascendancy to the throne he begged the royal women of the court to petition Akbar's forgiveness. Akbar indeed, as customary in his past actions, forgave Salim and presented him with his own turban as a sign that Akbar still intended to pass his throne to Salim without question.

Encouraged with his success to gain the women's support of his efforts, and Akbar's seemingly firm confirmation of succession, Salim returned to his addicted behavior. Using heavy amounts of opium and alcohol, during a military expedition to Rajasthan, Salim rebelled, broke military protocol, and left his army stranded ten miles across the Jamuna. Akbar did not hesitate to have Salim arrested and through swift military action had him thrown into solitary confinement where he was forced to face the hardships of fighting his addictions. Almost dying from the ordeal, Salim reevaluated his rebellious nature and knew beyond a shadow of a doubt that his father was still a gigantic power and one with whom he could not compete.

Akbar was emotionally bereft when contemplating Salim's personality. The only son left to him was filled with cowardice and treachery. How could the hope for his legacy carry on after his death? The only faithful people Akbar realized who were standing in dedicated service by his side, where Abdur Rahim, the present Khan-i-Khanan, Mirza Aziz Koka, and Raja Man Singh. They unanimously did not approve of Salim's succession. They strongly opposed his ascendancy to the throne asserting his addicted behavior as a great stumbling block. They pointed to his cruelty to his own people as poor attributes for a King. They all knew of his intolerance toward the other religious groups living in the area and felt that Salim would never carry forth Akbar's spiritual ideals. They also saw Salim's continual bouts of rebellion against Akbar as a sign of inherent weakness and supported Khusrau's supersession. The faithful elders saw Khusrau as intellectual, very well mannered and one who could infuse the ideals and policies of religious tolerance that Akbar had installed in the fading *Din-I-Illahi*.

On September 22nd, 1605 Akbar fell seriously ill. The altercations between Salim and himself were intensifying and his doctor, Hakim Ali, it appeared, could find no remedy. Salim finally came to his dying father and entered the bedchamber of a heavy cushioned diwan. Finally bowing in submission and reverence he awaited his father's last words. A few tense moments passed between father and son, then Akbar, with tears pouring down his fading eyes, again placed the royal turban on Salim's head and gave him the sword of Timur. With these actions the succession of the Timurid line was validated.

Outside the fort, thousand of devoted followers could be heard wailing in sorrow at the inevitable lose of their cherished benefactor. On October 17th, 1605 Akbar died. He was carried on a palanquin (*jenazah*) by the grandsons who he loved and favored above that of his own son, and was taken to a tomb which he partly designed. Akbar was the first Mogul Emperor buried on Hindustani soil. During his life, Akbar was a visionary of unified coexistence and in his burial he carried forth the same ideals. His most exquisite tomb was built at Sirkandra, six miles from Agra and although stripped of its glorious beauty during periodic insurgent uprisings, it can be visited today.

Salim took the throne as Jahangir and it is recorded that he eventually abstained from all drugs and alcohol becoming a Dervish who distrusted his senses. He also held in reverence the wise counsel of the Sufis and remained loyal to his father by trying to carry many of the ideals forward in the manner that he was able to understand them. Although Salim's capacity for tolerance in the manner that Akbar understood it within inter-religious dialogue, never moved forward in his reign. He became a far more conservati practicing Muslim than Akbar, as did Khusrau who succeeded Salim. He remained the Christian, Zoroastrian and Hindu population respecting their Holy Days bu orthodox tendencies lacked Akbar's intrinsic fairness.

The Jahangir had painful difficulties with his father during his lifetime but later in Salim's reign he credits Akbar with lavish memories and praise saying,

> "The good qualities of my revered father, are beyond the limit of approval and the bounds of praise. If books were composed with regard to his commendable dispositions, without suspicion of extravagance, and he be not looked at as a father would be by his son, even then but a little out of much could be said."[106]

Akbar's greatest disappointment and failure was that his sons could not carry forward his dreams and he, as their father, was unable to set the model for them at their most influential age, as he too struggled with his own addictions throughout his life.

---

[106] Burke, 1989, P.211

AKBAR'S LEGACY

There should be no doubt in the mind of the reader how remarkably futuristic Akbar was in his attempted ideas installed in his new religion *(Sulk-i-kul)* which promoted religious tolerance. Taking the Imperial responsibility of a complex series of state issues at the age of thirteen, never before had a Mogul conqueror brought forth into the community such worthy ideals of cultural and religious fairness and magnanimous distribution of wealth to the citizens of his empire. Even as a boy-King he began his ascent out of the cruel archetype found in the Timurid legacy of Mogul warrior Emperors. This fact alone is astounding because the empire that he inherited was ravaged by wars and frequent changes of government and internal tensions among citizens of different races, religions and cultures.

Akbar's bloody conquests, which have purposely not been highlighted in the corpus of this treatise, have only peripherally been mentioned for the purpose of giving insight into his personality and spiritual quest. These circumstances would clearly show what an astounding fearless warrior he became particularly if motivated by his lustful pursuits. This fact is confirmed in many historic documents describing his battles and the political intrigues that surrounded them. As a leader of his people, and one who was connected to a dynasty of conquerors, he was expected to win greater territory and protect his borders from counter attack at all times.

This treatise deals with his state of mind and heart when under the Sufi influence that supported his established *Din-i-Illahi*. The implications of a warrior king living in the same person as a humble spiritual seeker of truth, is axiomatic and very close to the truth about his nature. My hope was to reveal the specific detailed accounts of his feelings and reasons for making the decisions that he wished to fulfill in his reign as a support to his spiritual choices that he wished to fulfill. The circumstances that are reflected here bring to light how he dealt with the uncertainty of change, expansion and tribal competition that threatened his leadership and how spiritual independence rose in his mind when betrayed by his closest family members. He chose to return to the battlefield throughout the years of his reign when he would have preferred the deep spiritual dialogue with his Sufi companions which was what his heart craved.

Taking into account the savage drama of his childhood experience on the battlefield witnessing the harsh realities of war and death of his father's army and those of his father's enemies, he managed to use these memories to divert many hostile actions that would provoke further breakage in important alliances. His fair judgment was developed in the atmosphere of the enduring Sufi impact that had influenced the Indian subcontinent for centuries.

The atrocities of war that he tried to escape in his futile rush to inebriation and lustful practices broke his resolve many times. However, in abundant possibilities which he found living in the wise men of Sufism, he regained his balance and offered a generous method to the people of his Empire of reconciliation and harmony.

His success as a ruler was astounding. His domestic policies brought honor and respect to Muslim ethics. He challenged fixated thinking and fundamentalist principles that crippled living a true spiritual life. He single handedly opened the door to what is now known as "interfaith" dialogue. He left behind a stable and flourishing empire and a system of administration that would rival the British Government's with one added and superb feature; he brought religious tolerance to an unprecedented height. Akbar's methods remained fairly well intact throughout his son's reign (the Jahangir) and that of his grandson (Shah Jehan who is credited for building the famous Taj Mahal) carrying further stability into two and a half centuries of Indian history. But the loss of his special charisma and Akbar's characteristic burning desire for knowledge and truth was his alone. He lived from his emotions and they were married to the heart of wide expanse of Sufi teachings offered by the great masters who surrounded him. It was his innate understanding of the Sufi teachings that was his most profound legacy that lives on today.

When dealing with these enemies he knew that, "God alone was perfect." He kept this spiritual realization on his "Shast," God is Great" *(Allah ho Akbar)* because he believed in the spiritual value of words which were sacred vibrations. He was firmly rooted in the idea that his royal seal *(shast)* would help him meet all obstacles in his life. Although he was highly criticized by his enemies, he could never show weakness nor did he wish to antagonize them for the sake of vanity. He simply prevented them from preparing a blow by removing them from his inner circle and the empire. He was never vindictive nor did he terrorize their well being. He simply did not want a lemon in the cream.

He saw his own imperfections and those of others and he knew above all reason that the Sufi teachings of the Universal Spirit of Guidance would direct the heart from within toward wisdom. He loved the great prophets of humanity and wished to learn everything they taught. His realization and secular methods of discursive investigation caused alarm in those who remained uninterested and who chose not to investigate outside their own doctrine.

The idea that the material world is not opposite to and apart from the Creator is a Sufi idea and this is given expression in the various passages quoted by Abul Fazl. To Akbar the world was only the manifestation of the Supreme Essence and they are both one and the same. Life cannot be divided into two compartments of religious/spiritual and worldly/material. Abul Fazl says, "*The Lover and the Beloved are in reality one; idle talkers speak of the Brahman as distinct from his idol. There is but one lamp in this house in the rays of which wherever I look a bright assembly meets me.*" According to Abul Fazl, this idea that extreme asceticism was quite unnecessary for a spiritual life and that the search after truth can be combined with work here in this world was an idea which was given to him by Akbar. Before he came into the Imperial presence he sought to be remote from the society around him and looked upon external circumstances as destructive of inwardness and limitation as opposed to absoluteness. Akbar taught him.

"That the work of the world, multifarious as it is, may yet harmonize with the spiritual unity of truth."[107]

Akbar's religious system brought in monotheism along with pantheism tracing its source to the Emperor's own heart impulses and ideas formed through analytic discussions and rationalizations researched in his study of religious scriptural texts and rituals. He supported a monotheistic view based on the inherent understanding of the Sufi's Zikar practice which they recited as their mantram, "There is no reality but the Divine", (*La illaha il 'Allah Hu*). To Akbar, the Divine could be known through many ways and living things. He worshipped the Sun all his life and believed in the formless images found in dreams and imagination. He acknowledged and loved the arts, notes in music and the intrinsic harmony in architecture. Like the Sufis and Indian Vedantist's, everything was an aspect of Divine manifestation including his own being. He firmly felt his Divine fiat was as the vicegerent in matters of State and Spirituality. Given the historic details of his charismatic powers, one would take his claim seriously. By evidence of what he contributed to the members in his empire and the interfaith ideals he proposed what he could certainly be called a Prophet/King of his time.

---

[107] Krishnamurti, 1961, P. 151, fn 1

Akbar's faithful court historian and beloved companion Abul Fazl wrote with elaborate details what he heard and saw in Akbar's courtly life. Abul Fazl's descriptions bring to life the copious decisions and struggles his King faced in the storm of difficulties and conflicts. Although scholars such as Badoani in his *Ain-i-Akbari*, and the Jesuit Christian father Monserrate in his *Commentary of His Journey to the Court of Akbar*, have argued over facts and descriptions in the Mogul empire under Akbar's reign, the *Akbar Nama* is the closest historic document that reveals Akbar, the man. The reason for this being that the Emperor was truly himself when spiritual companions that reflected the light in his own heart surrounded him. Abul Fazl, Faizee and Sheikh Mubarak were those companions that celebrated with the other Sufi masters Akbar's high powered, vital and deeply spiritual destiny. When all is said and done it is Abul Fazl's accounting that gives us the most detailed insight into this King.

In the many Christian, and Islamic based historians and the documents of Akbar's court, there continues to be a mistaken fact that Akbar tried to undo the Muslim strong-hold in India. Through his attempts to establish tolerance among the many different religions in his empire he set up misgivings in the hearts of the orthodox. They wanted him as their own, as he was born a Muslim, but he challenged and questioned all religious scripture. Akbar's characteristic to rationalize was observed, especially by Badaoni, as being inconsistent with being a Muslim. No person has the authority to question statements in the Qur'an or Hadith's nor anything handed down by posterity concerning the personality of the Prophet (*SAAwS*). This fact was firmly agreed upon by the orthodox pundits (*'ulama*). Akbar simply could not follow anyone or any religion blindly. He was fiercely against the outward observances that others followed without questioning them; and he was impatient with ritual prescriptions that had no meaning but outwardly conformed to popular opinions. The truth is, he belonged to every religion but he never allowed any doctrine to jail him in a confined creed. His belief supported the true essence of Islam, which was Unity (Tawhid), and as some historians have said, he wished that members surrounding the Prophet had written a commentary on his own words during his lifetime.

This would have limited the scope for contradictions, later found in communities of Muslims.[108]

After witnessing that the community in general fell back on old patterns of worship and ritual, hardliners remained firm in Akbar's court. Feeling the need for discipline he commanded obedience to his dictates and observances by his inner circle, (*Din-I-Illahi*) to follow his instructions and attend debates with many representatives of religious streams. He felt he needed to force dialogue for the purpose of opening minds to critical thinking. Akbar gave instructions not as a dictator but rather as an authority that ordains intelligence and reason as the means to lift the community out of self-inflicted exile. That exile was reflected in those ideologies that kept one from respecting and sharing this life together as brothers and sisters of the same Creator. Akbar believed that this sharing of perspective kept the heart open and fundamental rigidities at abeyance.

Akbar rejected the traditional Muslim ideas of redemptive justice and punishment in infernal regions and reward in Paradise. He also rejected the Christian ideas of Resurrection and Judgment. He rather believed in the transmigration of souls and the gradual evolution which one takes from lower forms to higher ones as spoken of by the great Sufi poet Jelaluddin Rumi. He believed that the Creator did not punish the creation. He felt all the trials and tribulations that were threatened upon the public by the pundits of all faiths were generated for the purpose of control over another. Akbar firmly believed that, "Allah who knows both what is hidden *(Batin)* and what is manifest *(Zahir)* have recourse to trials. He rather felt, as Abul Fazl confirms, that the rational mind and soul of an individual was a subtle divine essence, separate from the body, having however, a peculiar union with the elemental form.[109] He faced nature as a guileless child in awe and reverence to the greatest order revealed in the laws of the universe. He ceased all anthropomorphic worship of deities and submitted entirely his determination to the perfect trust and ultimate triumph of righteousness ennobling all living things.

---

[108] Krishnamurti, 1961, P.163
[109] Recorded by Badaoni in the Ain-I-Akbari III, as being Abul Fazl's perspective on Akbar's belief. P.391.

Akbar formulated a fully scripted spiritual plan for a life of prayer, devotion to others, rituals and meditations. He saw great benefit coming to his society if members that composed the different cultural groups would listen to each other's perspective and gain from a greater eclectic insight. He became alerted to the viperous outbursts of the religious pundits who became fixated on their own perspectives and ungenerous to others. This fact alerted him to the dangers in religious fundamentalism and the insidious contamination of egotism when positions of power gave preference to those in leadership.

Zoroastrians inspired him, Jains, Brahmans, Christians and above all, nature itself. Whether he followed any of these religions or all of them gives a faithful student a good start into further research. It is certain as Krishnamurti declares, "He had in fact become sufficiently unorthodox to create misgivings in the hearts of the orthodox *'ulama* while he retained as much of Islam as of the other religions."[110] Although criticized by many religious historians as being inconsistent as a Muslim, he bore only respect for the teachings in Qur'an. It is true that Akbar refused literalist interpretation and always sought to look deeper into the meaning of prophetic revelation. Akbar used every moment for self-examination, and under the watchful eye of Sufi Masters, he devoted many days in retreat (*Khilvat*) at the holy shrine (*Dargah*) of Hazrat Khwaja Moineddin Chisthi.

Since the Sufis refuse to idealize a personality but rather turn their attention to the practice of effacement (*fana*) in the Divine ideal, hence the need for vigorous discipline and devotional attitudes. His many pilgrimages to the Dargah of this Sufi master reminded him of the Great Mystery, the Creator and the important responsibilities he had as a leader to his people. Veneration for all of life was Akbar's primary faith. He even gave up eating meat because of the deeper understanding that dawned on him relating blood as the principle of life itself. He realized that ceasing meat eating was saving life.

Although inspired to change his attitudes he never forced members of his empire to follow his example as a constant discipline. He spoke continually of the differences

---

[110] Krishnamurti, 1961, P.159

between formal conformity to a religion and a real living faith. However he did make rules that reflected a kinder relationship to the animals and offered sufficiently valid reasons why people could find abundant provision elsewhere.

Akbar left behind a prodigious fortune coined in the billions of equivalent dollars. He was neither miserly nor affected by the love of money. His skill at administration was masterful in bringing and sending resources without extorting oppressive methods. He was a superb manager and guarded his resources with great care. Charity and alms giving was a very large part of Akbar's legacy and he offered generous stipends to those who where in his employ.

Akbar built up a mighty and glorious empire which brought prosperity and hope to the entire Indian subcontinent. He beautified every portion of the land under his dominion with vegetation, agricultural projects, large lakes, and abundance of animals, birds and fish. This prosperity endured for almost a century until, after his death, the anarchic tendencies inherently existing in the multi-religious polity and racial complexes arose once again.

Akbar was a genius. His contribution toward the ideals of interfaith coexistence was a cure for afflicted quarrelsome tendency found in humanity throughout the ages. As religious followers fought other religious followers, Akbar was setting the stage for the future for peaceful interfaith dialogue. His vision of tolerance was paradoxically his lasting contribution to the conception of one country when the age of nationalism was born during the reign of Queen Victoria. If Akbar had not brought the divided nation together the British might have treated the separate units poorly.[111]

For this Mogul King a spiritual life was an active life of good works. He held true to the Sufi teachings that emphasized how the Perfect Prophet (*SAAwS*) led his disciples to wisdom and knowledge and through his self-directed labor they learned to understand the precepts that God had ordained for the creature and the created. He wanted to investigate

---

[11] Srivastava, 1998, P.228

and deepen his spiritual knowledge and learn what was inherently similar in all paths making him the most unusual interfaith student and Mogul Emperor in the annuals of history.

Akbar-Bibliography

Rizvi, Saiyid Athar Abbas. The History of Sufism in India. New Delhi: Munshiram Manoharlal, Pvt. Ltd. 1975, 1978, 1997.

Gibb, H.A.R. and J.H. Kramers (Eds.) Shorter Enclyclopaedia of Islam. Leiden: E.J. Brill, 1961

Embree, Ainslie T. (Ed) Enclopaedia of Asia History, Vol.I. New York: Charles Scribner's, Sons, 1988.

Khan, F.A. Journal of Royal Asiatic Society, The Nobility under Akbar and the Development of his Religious Policy, 1968, pages 29-36.

Bhattacharya, Sachehindananda. Dictionary of India History. Calcutta: University of Calcutta, 1967.

Foltz, Richard C. Mughal India and Central Asia, Karachi: Oxford University Press, 1998

Binyon, Lawrence. Akbar, Great Britian: Peter Davis Ltd. and University Press, Edinburgh, 1932.

Fazl, Abul. (Tr. From Persian by H. Beveridge) The Akbar Nama-History of the Reign of Akbar including an Account of his predecessors. Volumes I, II, & III. Delhi: Ess Ess Publications, 1973, 1977.

Fazl, Abul. Akbar-Nama, Lahore, Pakistan: Sheikh Mubarak Ali Publishers and Booksellers, 1875, 1975

Khan, Iqtidar Alam (Ed.) Akbar and His Age. New Delhi: Northern Book Center, 1999.

Allami, Abul Fazl. (Tr. H. Blochmann) Ain-i Akbari. Delhi: Aadiesh Book Depot, 1871, 1965.

Burke, S.M. Akbar The Greatest Mogul. New Delhi: Munshiram Manoharlal Publishers Pvt. Ltd. 1989

Lal, Muni. Akbar. New Delhi: Vikas Publishing House Pvt. Ltd. 1980.

Qandhiri, Muhammad Arif. Tarikh-i –Akbari. (Tr.Tasneem Ahmad). Delhi: Pragati Publications, 1993.

Khan, Ahsan Raza. Chieftans in the Mughal Empire During the Reign of Akbar. Delhi: Indian Institute of Advanced Study, 1977.

Srivastava, Kamal. S. Two Great Mughals, Akbar and Aurangzeb. Varanasi: Sangeeta Prakashan, 1998.

Al-Badaoni (Badauni), Abdul Qadir Ibn-i-Muluk Shah. *Muntakhabut Tawarikh*, Vol. I (Tr.George S.A.Ranking). Patna: B.P. Ambashthya, 1973.

Begg, W.D. The Holy Biography of Hazrat Khwaja Muinuddin Chishti. Holland: East-West Publications, Fonds B.V. 1956, 1977.

Shah, Indries. The Way of the Sufi. London: Arkana-Penquin Group Publishers, 1968, 1974, 1990.

Hoyland, J.S. (Translated from the Original Latin). The Commentary of Father Monserrate, S.J. On his Journey to the Court of Akbar. London: Humphrey Milford, Oxford University Press, 1922.

Krishnamurti, R. Akbar-The Religious Aspect. Baroda: Maharaja Sayajirao University of Baroda Press, 1961.

Ambashthya, B.P Contributions on Akbar and the Parsees. Patna:Janaki Prakashan at Tapan Printing Press, 1976.

Dadbar, Abolghasem. Iranian in Mughal Politics and Society-1606-1658. New Delhi: Gyan Publishing House, 1999.

Nizami, Khaliq Ahmad. Akbar & Religion. Delhi: Idarah-I-Adabutat-I-Delli at Jayyed Press, 1989.

Smith, Vincent, A. Akbar-The Great Mogul-1542-1605. Delhi: S. Chand & Co. 1958, 1962, 1966.

Hughes, Thomas Patrick. Dictionary of Islam. Delhi: Oriental Publishers, 1973.

Eliade, Mircea. A History of Religious Ideas. Volume 3 –From Mohammad to theAge of Reforms. Chicago: The University of Chicago Press, 1982.

Khan, Hazrat Inayat. The Mysticism of Sound-Sufi Message Volumns – II. London: Barrie and Jenkins, 1960, 1969, 1970.

Al-Ghazzali, Sheikh Muhammad. The Thematic Commentary on the Qur'an. London: The International Institute of Islamic Thought, 2000.

Siddiqi, Muhammad Zubayr. Hadith Literature-Its Origin, Development & Special Features. Cambridge: The Islamic Text Society, 1993.

Esposito, John L. (Ed.) The Oxford History of Islam. Oxford: Oxford University Press, 1999.

www.ingramcontent.com/pod-product-compliance
Lightning Source LLC
Chambersburg PA
CBHW041820090426
42811CB00009B/1043